I0007042

The Elements of Computing Style

200+ Tips for Busy Knowledge Workers

Diomidis Spinellis

The Elements of Computing Style

200+ Tips for Busy Knowledge Workers

Diomidis Spinellis

This book is for sale at http://www.computingstyle.com

This version was published on 2014-08-27

ISBN 978-1500972097

Many of the designations used by manufacturers and sellers to distinguish their products are claimed as trademarks. Where those designations appear in this book, and the author was aware of a trademark claim, the designations have been printed with initial capital letters or in all capitals.

The author and publisher have taken care in the preparation of this book, but make no expressed or implied warranty of any kind and assume no responsibility for errors or omissions. No liability is assumed for incidental or consequential damages in connection with or arising out of the use of the information or programs contained herein.

©2013 - 2014 Diomidis Spinellis

Contents

Preface

For me, a habitual misspeller, scrawler, hopeless at remembering things, and embarrassingly bad with figures, technology freak, my association with computers has been redemptive. Through them I've somehow, against all hope, presented to the world a persona that manages to hide these horrible problems, as long that is, as I have a keyboard near me (which is almost all the time). I have thus realized the tremendous power of computer technology as a personal productivity-enhancing tool. At the same time, I've also observed that many knowledgeable, intelligent, and highly-effective people, maybe like you, fail to take advantage of the computing technology's full potential.

When I see you working on your laptop, as a colleague on a desk beside me or as a stranger in an airport lounge, I can't help but noticing that with some small changes you can save a lot of time and effort while also getting better results. I've therefore collected more than 200 pieces of advice in this little book, hoping that you can read them when you're less busy, and look them up when you really need them.

Some of the advice is really important, other borders on the frivolous. My collection is eclectic rather than all-encompassing: I've put together those elements that have invariably served me well over the years, the gems that I really wanted to share with you. You'll see that, like compound interest, their combined effect on your productivity will be impressive.

Let me finish by clarifying that although following my advice will not make you a computer professional (sorry), you'll still be a lot better than many who, by my experience, claim they are.

Diomidis Spinellis

1. General

1.1 If it doesn't work, try it again

An electrical, a mechanical, a chemical, and a computer engineer were in a car traveling in the hot desert. Predictably, in the middle of the vast emptiness the dreadful "check engine" indicator lit on the dashboard and a minute later the car's engine shut down. The mechanical engineer quickly blamed the desert's sand, suggesting a thorough engine cleanup. The electrical engineer retorted that vibrations probably loosened a sparkplug connection; reseating the connectors should fix the problem. "Don't be so sure", responded the chemical engineer, "this is an air-fuel mixture problem. We should continue our journey at night, when the air will be cooler." The computer engineer, having politely waited for his colleagues to finish, was now ready to offer his professional opinion. "Listen guys. Modern cars are run by tens of computer processors. I'm sure this is a software problem, and fixing it is trivial," he said smugly. "Let's just get out of the car and in again."

There's a lot of wisdom in this story. Last summer, after maneuvering for about ten minutes to unpark our new car from a tight uphill parking place, I sensed that something was wrong with the engine. Its sound was distinctively wrong, resembling that of an old diesel-powered boat. Worse, once we were out of the traffic, I realized that the engine simply refused to run above 2,000 revolutions per minute. Changing gears, or flooring the gas pedal didn't help. The car continued to crawl slowly forward at its leisurely pace, with other cars honking behind, and small motorcycles overtaking us. Our vacation was turning into a nightmare. Finding an engineer to fix this strange problem in a remote Greek island was going to be challenging, returning home with two toddlers without the car, impossible. Then my wife, a computer engineer by training, offered the solution I was ashamed to contemplate. "Just turn off the engine, and turn it on again," she said. Sure enough, a minute later the car was purring happily driving us home.

So, the most important piece of advice you should remember from this book is that if something computer-related doesn't work, you should retry it, preferably starting from a clean slate. How do you start from a clean slate? If you're running a program on a PC, exit the program and start it again. If that fails, shut down your computer and restart it. (Warning: this must be a complete shut down, putting your computer to sleep or hibernating it is not enough). If the problem is in your broadband connection turn the modem off and on again. The same goes for your cell phone, your tablet, your music player, or your TV set-top box.

In some cases, switching the device off doesn't really turn off the computer hiding inside, so you'll have to resort to harsher measures. You may need to unplug the mains power or remove the battery. On many laptops you may need to hold down the power button continuously for as long as ten seconds. Some appliances even have a tiny "reset" button hidden on their back or underneath. Pressing this button sometimes results in the device loosing its settings or the data you've stored in it, but it can be an effective last resort for a device you've thought was broken. The alarm radio in my bedroom requires this treatment every couple of years—unfortunately a time span long enough for me to forget the existence and location of its reset button.

You may ask: "How can a supposedly accurate and infallible computer respond in different ways to the same command?" The truth is that computers are nothing but infallible. The software they run, from your word processor to your cell phone's menu, is full of defects, known in our trade as "bugs". These may be harmless, resulting for instance in overlapping images on a web page, or very expensive, such as the metric unit mix-up that destroyed NASA's Mars Climate Orbiter. The effects of many bugs are not immediately obvious, but remain hidden in the computer's memory. Therefore, restarting a program or the computer, will often clear that problem allowing you to proceed with your work.

Many problems also occur due to external factors that may have changed next time we retry an operation. A speck of dust on an unreadable CD may shift its position allowing you to read it, or a broken computer that hosted a web page you couldn't access can be up again ready to send you that page. This is especially true for network connections, which are both fragile (many are literally made of glass) and constantly monitored by the telecom companies. Therefore, when you experience a network-related problem, go walk your dog and try again. Important network resources—say the front page of Google—should recover in minutes; for less critical services—for instance, the mail system of a small company—you may have to wait a day or two.

Of course, if a local problem persists it might be worth looking for the underlying cause, by asking an expert, or trying alternative actions (see item 1.2). Restarting a program or a computer many times a day is certainly no fun, and it's not something you should tolerate as a normal work procedure. Nevertheless, restarts are a tried and true solution with a sound scientific basis followed by amateurs and pros alike. Computer restarts are even prescribed in many cockpit procedures; ask the captain of a large aircraft. So next time a computer misbehaves, simply restart it.

1.2 If it doesn't work, try it in a different way

You can deal with any problem in three ways: you solve it, you ignore it, or you work around it. Unless you support computers for a living (in which case it's rather worrying that you're reading this book) troubleshooting computer problems is not a productive way to spend your time. So unless you can ignore a problem (for instance, it's not worth fretting about a blank line appearing between two footnotes in an internal memo) your best option for dealing with computer problems is to work around them. Alexander the Great famously followed this strategy when asked to untie the Gordian knot by cutting through it, and then marched on acquiring fame and fortune. Following his lead sounds like a sensible idea.

Here are examples of alternative approaches for solving some common problems.

- If a document prints in a funny way, try printing it on another printer. If you can't access another printer, try converting your document into PDF format (many programs provide this option), and then print that. Alternatively, you could try using a different printer driver for your printer. For instance, most high-end printers come with so-called PCL and Postscript printer drivers. If one driver doesn't print your diagrams as you expect them, try installing and using the other.
- If you can't paste an image you copied from a web page onto your presentation, try pasting it into an image-processing program, and from there to your presentation. Or try saving it into a file, and then inserting the file into your presentation.
- If a keyboard shortcut doesn't work (say ALT-F for opening the File menu) try navigating with the mouse. And the opposite: if you can't do something with the mouse, try a keyboard shortcut.
- If your broadband connection is down (and you can't wait for it to come up again), try connecting to the internet through your cellphone's data connection.
- If the projector breaks down during a presentation, bring the audience to the front rows and use your laptop's screen. (At least you'll be compensated for the back pain of lugging that

large screen around.) Or, distribute the presentation to the participants through an email or a USB stick so they can follow it from their laptops (or so you'd like to think). Alternatively, if you don't want to have anything more to do with the computer technology that failed you, simply photocopy and distribute the slide printouts you've (hopefully) brought with you.

- If you can't send or receive an email through your regular email provider, try using one of the free email services, such as Gmail, Hotmail, or Yahoo! Mail. Or, use the phone, or just walk to that other person's desk.
- If a web page doesn't work as expected with a particular browser (unfortunately some sites are only tested with a single one) try using a different one.
- If an application refuses to open a document with strange-looking characters in its name (e.g. `Růžičková.docx`) try giving the document a simpler name. Computers can get confused by weird accents as much as you do.

1.3 Search for the least common term

No matter if you're searching for a phrase in your document, a web page, or an email message, if you've got various terms by which you think you could find the item you're looking for, choose those that are the least common.

For instance, if you're searching for details about the the nineteenth century explorer Jedediah Smith, don't even dream about entering his surname in a search engine. Smith is the most common family name in most English-speaking countries, representing more than 1% of their inhabitants, and (through a strange phenomenon that has left statisticians dumbfounded) more than 20% of people checking into hotels. On the other hand, searching for "Jedediah" on Google will give you the corresponding Wikipedia web page as the top result.

The same applies when you're searching for a phrase in a large document. If you want to locate the phrase "The course of true love never did run smooth" in Shakespeare's *A Midsummer Night's Dream*, searching for "love" will cost you a bit, having you go through twelve other instances of the word, before you land on the phrase you're looking for (this is what typically happens when you're searching for love). However, if you search for less common (for this play) words, such as "course" or "smooth" you'll locate the phrase immediately.

1.4 RTFM, GIYF

RTFM stands (in polite language) for "read the fine manual". Let's be honest; we never read the documentation that comes with a program or a device. Therefore, we tend to forget that the answer we're looking for may be waiting for us, if we just take the time to read the fine manual (or nowadays the online help). Most programs have this available through a menu titled *Help* or a button with a question mark on it.

Another initialism that can help us when we're stuck is GIYF: Google is your friend. Type in Google's search box your problem (e.g. "How do I search for a file in Windows") or the parts of the error message that hit you ("circular reference warning"). Google will kindly oblige with countless web pages—some of them may actually be helpful.

2. Work Habits

2.1 Finish one task before proceeding to the next

"Thrashing" is the technical term for a computer that's spending so much time juggling various tasks, that it has little time to actually work on them. Well, guess what, we humans can suffer from the same problem.

Researchers from the University of California at Irvine have found that office workers switch the task they're working on once every 12 minutes on average. Each interruption can potentially start a new task. Accumulating those tasks on your desktop's surface (say a few unrelated worksheets, a couple of documents, some more open web pages, and an email reply) results in an environment that's difficult to navigate effectively. The same researchers found that office workers typically juggle about ten different tasks at the time.

Because your desktop's and toolbar's surface is limited, crowding it with unrelated items will have you spending unproductive time navigating between them. Therefore, try to minimize the tasks you leave open on your desktop, by finishing each task before moving on to the next one. If you can't finish a task, adopt a mechanism for hiding tasks that still need your attention under the proverbial carpet. For instance, you can create a folder where you keep shortcuts to documents you're working on, or a corresponding mail folder. Just don't leave them open on your desktop.

2.2 Leave work unfinished

There's a case to be made for leaving your work unfinished. If you're writing something substantial, it's often difficult to kick-start your writing; a condition known as the writer's block. In such a case, the most difficult time of the day is the morning, when you stare into the screen trying to regain your train of thought.

A way around this problem is to leave your work in the evening in a dramatically unfinished state. Stop in the middle of a paragraph or even in the middle of a sentence. Completing this small part will be relatively easy, because the preceding parts will be there to guide you. Once you complete the missing part, moving on will be a lot easier. First, you will have overcome the fear of becoming blocked, and, second, your brain will have revved up to the speed required to continue working productively.

2.3 Keep multiple work queues

In item 2.1 you saw that having too many items in your head can be counterproductive due to the cost of context switching. However, when you're so busy that you need to work in any place you are, you can increase the efficiency of your work by keeping a moderately large selection of pending tasks. This allows you to find an optimal match between a task and the type of work you can do at a given moment.

Let me clarify. Tasks that pass through your hands differ in their requirements on concentration, time, location, and facilities. By juggling around tasks from a rich selection you can ensure that you often get the chance to match a task to your work environment. Consider, for example, requirements on concentration. It would be foolish to spend the quite early-morning hours in your office spell-checking a document, or coming up with a complex negotiation strategy at a busy airport gate. Working on those tasks the other way round makes a lot more sense. (Unless, that is, the people you will negotiate with are loudly discussing *their* strategy while they wait to board.)

The following table identifies some typical work environments you may find yourself in and corresponding examples of types of tasks you can try to keep at hand. For some types of tasks it may make sense to create specific mail or file folders, for instance "To Read", "Home", "Office", "Regional Office", "Headquarters", or "Podcasts". The point to efficient multitasking is to match each task as closely as possible to the available work environment. Therefore, plan ahead to have appropriate tasks available for upcoming work environments.

Work Environment	Suitable Tasks
Low concentration; interruptible: Plane; airport gates; train; ferry; waiting for an appointment; recovering from jet-lag; eating alone; TV or children playing in the background	Sort email; take care of bureaucratic chores; organize and annotate photographs; experiment with new software; web surfing; improve the layout of charts and figures; give your presentations a face-lift
Medium concentration: Work office (during work hours); home office (when others are awake)	Flesh-out an already outlined document; tactical planning; create charts from existing data; answer routine emails; copy-edit printed text
High concentration: Home office (when others are asleep); work office (very early or late in the day)	Create an outline for a new document; strategic planning; devise and troubleshoot complex spreadsheets; interpret charts and figures

Work Environment	Suitable Tasks
Broadband access: Work; home; near Wi-Fi hotspots	Download email; web-based research; work on shared documents; access corporate databases; download podcasts; contact friends and colleagues through social networking sites; catch up with older tasks that required broadband access; keep up with the news
Lack of internet access: In more areas than you'd like	Organize files; write reports; read books and articles;
Proximity in an area: A specific building or office	Meet people; distribute material; fetch/send out postal mail; sign paper documents; file paper documents; return loaned items
No laptop: Bus; traveling very light; beach; mountain	Read journals, books, and magazines; printed or photocopied documents
Unable to read: Car; bus; waiting in a queue	Listen to podcasts

2.4 Plan, measure, and report your work

You have a big task, say writing or reviewing a 100 page report, in front of you. How can you ensure that you'll finish it on time? Three simple steps will get you there.

First, plan your work. Estimate its size; any measure, such as the number of pages, lines, or words will do. Pad up that number to take into account unforeseen work. Also set the completion date and calculate the number of available work days. Pad that number slightly down to plan for unanticipated events that might disturb your work pace. By dividing the work's size by the available time, you'll know how much work you must complete each day; for instance, writing 600 words or reviewing 12 pages.

Second, at the end of each day, measure the work you performed. All word-processors contain tools for measuring words and other elements. So far so obvious. The crucial part of this recipe is the third step.

At the end of each day, prepare a short (1–2 line) report indicating the work you performed on that day and the remaining work. You can easily automate this task by creating a spreadsheet where you plugin the number from the previous step. Email that report to your boss, your colleagues, or your subordinates, and also copy yourself. It doesn't matter who will get the report, the point is that you'll know that somebody is monitoring your progress. Each day a copy of the previous day's report in your mailbox will show you how you're slowly but steadily progressing toward your goal, and it will also remind you to complete your day's allocation.

I've used this method successfully to complete two books (including this one) and a few papers with tight deadlines. In one case the reports went to my managing editor, for this book I emailed the reports to graduate students I supervised. Both approaches worked wonders. Here is a sample report for this book.

```
Subject: Computing Style progress
Date: Thu, 1 Nov 2007 04:09:10 +0200 (EET)
From: Diomidis Spinellis <dds@example.com>
To: bob@example.com, alice@example.com
CC: dds@example.com


Progress Summary


Yesterday I had completed 34 of the 162
items (21.0 percent of the total). Today I
have completed 36 of the 163 items (22.1
percent of the total).
```

2.5 Don't leave it for the last minute

The amount of work modern computers perform with dizzying speed and unmatched precision distracts us from their complexity. For instance, the computational power I used on my laptop for typing this paragraph exceeds the computations that the Apollo Guidance Computer made during the 1967 lunar descent. The downside of this abundance of processing power is the myriad unpredictable ways a modern computer can fail. Worse, recovery from (the fortunately rate) failures is often beyond our control, requiring time-consuming repairs, vendor fixes, or patient troubleshooting.

Therefore, *avoid relying on a computer close to a deadline*. Work well in advance leaving ample time for dealing with contingencies. Corrupted files, program crashes, broken broadband connections, empty printer cartridges, and failed hard disks are facts of life. Don't let them escalate into crises by allowing them to occur near a pressing deadline.

"But countless of organizations depend on computers day in and day out", I hear you wonder. "Why can they get away with it, and I can't?" The answer is simple. Despite superficial similarities, there's a vast difference between the personal computing you perform on your desktop and that taking place in the computing rooms of banks, airlines, and internet companies. These rely on special hardware and software, redundant computers and network connections, on-site experts, and expensive vendor support contracts to solve problems before their clients even realize they occurred. You and I don't have this luxury and must therefore schedule ample time for solving the inevitable computer problems. This allows us to benefit from the magic-like productivity boost of modern computing, without having at our disposal Google's site reliability engineering support.

2.6 Comment your work

Mention the word "comments" to a group of computer programmers and a lively discussion will erupt. In programs comments are explanatory text that help programmers navigate around the code. As a non-programmer you can also benefit from comments. You can add them to word-processing documents, spreadsheets, and presentations to clarify how you derived what you wrote.

For instance, in a document, a comment you attach to a table can contain the title of the report or the web site where you found the corresponding data. If you need to verify it or revise it in the future, it will be easy to go back to the source. In a spreadsheet you might write a comment to explain how a particular formula you wrote actually works. And in a presentation you might use comments (there they go by the name "notes") for additional material you'll use during the presentation's delivery.

Many applications support comments through a menu command such as *Insert – Comment*. If the application you're using doesn't support comments, you can keep them in a separate file, stored in the same folder as the document you're working on. Read more about this tactic in item 2.7.

2.7 Keep note files with your work

Let's face it. Not all computer-based tasks are easy. Sometimes to achieve a particular effect you need to delve into deep, well-hidden, and sometimes sadistically misnamed menus, or enter obscure commands. Keeping a note file detailing the particular command sequence can be a timesaver next time you need to repeat these actions. This is particularly useful for tasks you perform repeatedly but infrequently, say a monthly or yearly report, or a product launch press release.

Write the instructions in a simple text file, keeping the same name across all projects (notes.txt is an appropriate name). A simple format with one line detailing the intended result, and another one describing the command sequence that achieved it is typically enough. When you document long-running non-repetitive projects, adding the current date to each entry provides you an additional way to navigate through your notes. Keep the notes file in each project's folder. Even if you'll need to go back to your notes in another context, the easiest thing to remember is the project where you originally performed that task.

2.8 Version before big changes

Safety-conscious rock climbers never climb an ascent to the top in one go. Instead, as they go up they secure their rope to the rock through protection devices, such as pitons and hooks, placed at periodic intervals. Thus, if they slip they will fall down to the last "protection" and not to the bottom. Do the same with your work. When you're happy with its state and you're about to embark on an extensive change, keep a copy of your work's current version. In this way, if the change goes bad, instead of loosing your work, you can backtrack to the "last known good" version and start again from there.

A convenient way for naming versions is to append _v (for version) and a two-digit number at the end of each file or directory. Thus, a document starts its life as report_v01 and continues as report_v02, and so on. The steps for creating the copy are simple.

1. Close the document from the application you're working on, or, even better, quit the application.
2. In the file manager (the Windows File Explorer or Apple's Finder) copy the document (*Edit – Copy*) and then paste it in the same folder (*Edit – Paste*).

3. Rename the document from, say, `Copy of report_v14` to `report_v15`.

If your project consists of many files, you can create a copy of the whole folder.

Some industries track successive versions using special software, known as a version control system. If your organization provides you with such software, and you're comfortable with it, more power to you.

Don't worry about the space these document versions occupy. Nowadays disk space is cheap and plentiful. Use it to make the, inevitable, accidents less damaging.

2.9 "Save As" before modifying

Often you create a document by opening an older one and modifying it as needed. For instance, you may write this month's progress report based on the report of the preceding month. This procedure can easily go wrong. You start working on the report, and at noon you save it to go for lunch. And thus you just clobbered the last month's report. To avoid this problem, immediately after opening the document you'll use as a template, save it with a new name. Another way to avoid this problem is to copy the document before opening it (see item 2.8).

If you realize the problem after you've saved the file, there's often still a way to recover. Undo all the changes you made (*Edit – Undo*), save the document, redo the changes (*Edit – Redo*), and then save it again with a new name.

2.10 Automate

Click-click click click-click-click, click-click click click-click-click, click-click click click-click-click is a telling pattern. It is evidence of a human serving a computer, performing a sequence of repetitive commands. It need not be so.

Whenever you find repeating yourself in front of a computer, consider automating the task. Use your head instead of your fingers. This switch will first of all reduce the risk of suffering from repetitive stress injury (RSI). If you can accomplish the effect of 100 keystrokes by typing 20 characters to specify a search and replace command, you'll have saved your fingers from the impact force of 80 keystrokes. Furthermore, by entering sophisticated commands, instead of repetitively typing, you remain attentive, rather than bored, and thus eliminate potential errors. Computers are a lot better than us humans in performing repetitive actions. Finally, and most importantly, each time you think of the way to automate a complex task by issuing an appropriate command you sharpen your mental skills. In contrast to your finite typing capacity, your mental skills seem to be infinitely expandable.

So, how can you automate a task? There are many ways, which differ from task to task and from application to application. Importantly, if a task you perform on a computer is repetitive, it will have irked many people, and a clever programmer will have devised a way to automate it. Through the invisible hand of the market that way is likely to have ended-up as a nifty feature in the application you're using. So when encountering a repetitive task, think, ask, and search for ways to automate it. Here are some general strategies.

The most common way to automate a task is through a special command. Consider having to replace hundreds of occurrences of the word "colour" in a long document with "color". Fortunately, all word processing programs offer a search-and-replace command. You specify the text to search ("colour"), the text to replace it with ("color"), and the program does the rest. Many more complex tasks can be automated. For instance, you can tailor mass letters and emails through the "Mailings" tab of Microsoft Word, or you can change the format of several graphics files in one go with the "Batch convert" command of Corel's PaintShop Pro.

If a program doesn't offer the command you're looking for, consider moving your data to another, more versatile program, and (maybe) back again. Read item 2.15 for more details.

Finally, a more sophisticated way involves the use of so-called scripting or macros. Although going into depth on this subject is beyond the scope of this book, the basic idea is that you provide the application with the instructions you want it to perform. You can then invoke the canned instructions whenever you want to execute the particular task. This is a form of programming, but do not let the concept frighten you. Non-programmers use macros all over the world to automate their work, and many are finding it a very enjoyable pastime. Indeed, some programs can even automatically record your actions into a macro, so you can program without ever looking at code (see item 18.5).

2.11 Spell check

Nowadays most programs will helpfully check your text's spelling. This is a mixed blessing, because your associates who find in your document glaring spelling errors, will realize that you care so little for its content, that you didn't even take the trouble to run the spell checker on it. They could well interpret this to mean that your document's ideas are also half-baked. Therefore, make it a habit to spell check your work before sending it off. Even if your spelling is perfect, use the spell checker to correct those inevitable typos.

Of course, if you really care about your document afterwards you'll correct it on paper (see item 2.12). However, running your text through the spell checker first will ensure that your correction efforts won't be distracted by trivial errors, so that you'll be able to focus on the essentials.

2.12 Correct on paper

Despite the niftiness of your application program and the clarity of your screen, correcting a document printed on paper will always be a more productive option. Once you pore over the sheets, you'll find that you'll uncover more errors, and that you can perform more thorough corrections. There are at least two reasons for this. First, a printed document is a lot crisper than its rendering on the screen. In addition, marking corrections on paper is considerably less distracting than fumbling with the keyboard and mouse.

To convince yourself of this, polish a document as best as you can on your computer's screen. Then print it out, and have another go at it. You'll be surprised at the number of improvements you'll still be able to make. So, when a document is important, don't pinch pennies (or CO_2 emissions): print it out, and correct it on paper. Once, twice, and again, until it's perfect.

2.13 Learn those correction symbols

Now that you're convinced that correcting documents on paper is the way to go (see item 2.12), invest some effort to learn the printer's correction symbols.[1] These provide you with a concise and standard notation to mark your changes. Having marked your changes on paper with these symbols, you can then easily apply them to your document, without having to guess what you meant by a particular correction. Even better, because this notation is widely documented and used, you can hand-out the corrected sheets and the tedious job of keying-in the changes to somebody else—an assistant or a convenient, ungrudging victim: the document's original writer.

---

[1]http://www.merriam-webster.com/mw/table/proofrea.htm

2.14 Mind map

The relationships between ideas are complex, so manipulating them on a linear document isn't productive and constrains your creativity. Next time you want to explore a knotty problem, try using a *mind map*. This is a diagram having a central idea or problem in its center with solutions, tasks, or related ideas connected with lines radiating from it. Each element can link to others, while colors, images, and diverse lettering amplify or categorize specific nodes. You can see some nice examples in Wikipedia's mind mapping entry.[2]

Although you can draw a simple one on paper, manipulating a mind map with specialized software can help you create much more elaborate diagrams. These can act as a roadmap or an idea repository, can be used for collaborating with a team, and can survive multiple revisions and reorganizations. Two free alternatives are the FreeMind[3] desktop software and the MindMup[4] online service.

2.15 Use each program for what it does best

In the 1980s, when PCs run at a leisurely pace of 4.77MHz (400 times slower than modern machines) and Lotus 123 was ruling the spreadsheet market, some people got so carried away with its power that they wrote letters and even small reports as spreadsheets. This says more about the ability of those people to twist a spreadsheet into a word processor, than Lotus's suitability for such a task. Nowadays, with integrated suites of office productivity programs being the norm, the stunt I described would be ridiculed, although

---

[2]https://en.wikipedia.org/wiki/Mind_mapping
[3]http://freemind.sourceforge.net/
[4]http://www.mindmup.com/

one does occasionally see a presentation delivered from a Word document.

Yet there's still room to work more productively, if you select the most appropriate tool for handling each task that you find difficult.

- Do you want to automate some extensive changes in a large email message? The search and replace command of your email program offers only the most primitive functionality, while the corresponding command of your word processor has many more features (see item 7.15). Therefore, copy the text to your word processor, perform the changes there, and paste it back to the email program.
- Does your word processor refuse to sort a table in a way you want? Copy the table to a spreadsheet, and manipulate there the cells to your heart's content.
- Do you want to print your document as multiple pages per sheet, but the program you're using doesn't offer such functionality? Convert the document into PDF, and then print it through Adobe Reader. The Reader's options under *File – Print – Page Sizing & Handling – Multiple* allow you to print multiple pages per sheet, and are so versatile that they will even allow you to specify a custom sheet layout.
- Can't create a nice picture in your word processor? Use a specialized image-drawing program, or try your luck with the program you use for creating presentations.

3. Searching the Web

3.1 Start your search with Wikipedia

At the time of writing, Google tracks more than twelve billion web pages. Google employs an astonishing amount of technical wizardry to locate the page you're looking for, but, nevertheless, it can sometimes fail. Therefore, when you're searching for information on something that's even slightly notable, start your search with Wikipedia. Although Wikipedia's accuracy and coverage are not perfect, it will often give you a concise overview of what you're looking for (including links to other relevant web sites) without the irrelevant hits often included in Google queries. So, no matter if you're searching for how the Tacoma Narrows Bridge collapsed, where mustard gas was first used, the cast of *Citizen Kane*, or the name of the orifice through which chickens lay their eggs, start with Wikipedia.

While you're using Wikipedia, consider contributing to an article in your area of interest. However, be careful: both browsing and contributing to Wikipedia can be highly addictive.

3.2 Find it next time

Wikipedia, despite its formidable depth and breadth (it contains more than two million articles), doesn't have the answer on everything. Sometimes you may be looking for information on a notable subject, and you may end up having to search on other web sites, or, heaven forbid, even a real library. However, if the information you've found is useful for you, and you're likely to need it again, there's a method to speed-up your search the next time you need it. Instead of tediously filing the information you found in the disorganized heap of your own documents, never to find it again, record it in the place where you looked in the first place: Wikipedia. That's right. Anyone can edit Wikipedia, so if what you found is verifiable encyclopedic content, simply add it to the corresponding article or in a new article. Then, next time you'll need that information, it will be on your fingertips.

3.3 Use phrase searches

By far the most useful "advanced" feature of some search engines, such as Google, is their ability to locate pages containing a phrase, not just individual words. To search for a phrase, simply include the words inside double quotes: `"from here to eternity"`.

There are a number of ways this feature can come handy.

Locate pages about specific people
Search for their name and surname as a phrase, for instance: `"Richard Wagner"`.

Target your search more effectively
Instead of searching for `led zeppelin`, which might give you pages about electronic lighting and flying machines, search for `"led zeppelin"`.

Locate again the web site from which you downloaded a particular document
Simply search for a phrase from that document.

Detect possible plagiarism
See the previous item.

Experimenting with the above searches on Google will show you that Google already takes the word proximity into account when ordering the search results. Nevertheless, the more specific you're in your search, the better search results you'll obtain.

3.4 Search sites through Google

Many web sites offer a search box. Surprisingly, the performance of this search facility is often inferior to that of Google's. Therefore, it's often better to ignore a site's search box and search it directly through Google. To coax Google to return pages coming from a specific site, simply add to your query the sequence `site:` *site name*. For instance, at the time of writing, searching on the New York Times web site for Gloria Mark— the researcher behind the information worker productivity research we discuss in item 2.1— returns as the first hit an article mentioning *Gloria* Davis and *Mark* Penn, and as the second one about Gloria Welles saying something about the pound hovering around the $2 *mark*. (Adding quotes around the name yields better results, but who wants to experiment with the quirks of every site's search engine.) On the other hand, typing into Google `site:nytimes.com gloria mark` returns as the first hit the New York Times article describing her work.

3.5 Search using an image

You see this really interesting picture in an obscure web site or a friend's profile, and you want to find more about it. This is how you can search for it.

- Right click on the image and select *Copy image URL* (on Google's Chrome browser) or *Copy image location* (on Mozilla Firefox).
- Go to the Google Images site.[1]
- Click on the camera icon on the right of the search box.
- Paste the image location you copied in the text input area (right-click in the input area and select *Paste*).
- Click on *Search by image*.

---

[1] http://images.google.com/

Google will come back with information about what you searched and a list of sites containing the specific image and related pictures.

If the image is already on your computer, you can simply upload it through the *Upload an image* option of the Google Images search window, and then search for it.

3.6 Let the web vote

You're unsure about the correct spelling of an actor's or top-manager's name, or the exact phrasing of an expression. Let the web vote, by running two Google searches, one for each alternative. The number of pages that match your query appears on the top right corner of the query's results page. The query with the highest number of hits is probably the correct one. Even if it isn't, you can console yourself knowing that you're on the same (misguided) boat with the majority.

3.7 Ask StackExchange

StackExchange[2] is a network of more than a hundred question and answer sites with 4.5 million users containing 8 million questions and (more importantly) 14 million answers. The topics covered by these sites range from mathematics, philosophy, and English language to video-gaming, sustainable living, and physical fitness. A system of voting for questions and answers plus reputation points and badges for contributors keeps the content helpful and relevant. Therefore, if your question's topic is covered by a StackExchange site, search in it for an answer. If you don't find one, register (it's free) and ask. Answers are often posted by experts only minutes later. As a token of your appreciation, consider contributing back to a StackExchange site a few answers on a topic you know.

---

[2]http://stackexchange.com/

3.8 Cast wide nets to locate an email address

Locating a person's email address should be as easy as opening a phone book. Sadly, as an ineffectual measure to prevent spam (see item 5.12), no such catalogs exist, so you have to work on your own. Start by searching for the person's name (in double quotes) on Google. From there navigate to pages that might contain the person's email address: a blog, a home page, a publication, a message sent to a public email list, or a social network page. If the name you're searching is too common, narrow down your search by adding the trailing parts of the company's internet address. For instance, search for `"john smith" "coca-cola.com"`. If you find something this person has written, look for the person's contact details at the beginning or end of the text. Also, navigate to the person's organization web site (e.g. their employer) and look for a contact list or a directory. Some organizations provide a searchable employee directory that's inaccessible to search engines, so you have to search there on your own. If you've found the person you're looking for on a social network, such as Facebook, Twitter, or LinkedIn, use that network to send them a message introducing yourself and asking for their email address. And, finally, don't forget the most obvious way: pick up the phone and ask around.

4. Web Tips and Tricks

4.1 The internet never forgets

So be careful what you post. Blog entries and your comments to other blogs, your profile on social networking sites, such as Facebook and LinkedIn, messages you post to mailing lists, and even exchanges through chat clients are probably archived somewhere. Future employees, colleagues, friends, relatives, and partners will find them, and judge you through them. Never post on the internet things you might one day regret (see item 13.2). And if you really have to discuss your fetish preferences online, do that under an alias.

4.2 Judge your online sources

We can all judge a restaurant without setting a foot in it. Its location, the lighting, the furniture, the tablecloths (or their absence), and the number of clients in (or their absence) it give us important clues. You can use similar clues for judging a web site, and this can save you from wasting time on a content-free site or embarrassing yourself by obtaining facts from a biased source.

Here are some signs for a trustworthy web page.

- It's associated with a respected organization (check the URL— item 4.3, if you landed there from a search)
- The site features a clean, professional, and user-friendly layout; easy navigation
- The site is mentioned in a number of other sites

- The site is associated with an educational, a research, or a reputable non-profit organization

And here are some warning signs.

- More adverts than useful content
- More links to other sites than useful content
- Overly flashy (and flashing) graphics and fonts
- A background image or color obscuring the text
- Spontaneously appearing popup windows
- Banners informing you that you've won the lottery
- Banners with scantily dressed girls (or guys)
- Links to a hodgepodge of irrelevant sites (ring tones, dating, credit reports, pharmaceutical products)

4.3 URLs are your friends

The text appearing on the navigation bar of your browser goes by the important-sounding name *uniform resource locator*, in short, URL. Just as a family's address allows you to locate their home, a URL will direct you to a web page. A postal address does more than direct you to a place. From it you can surmise the city where that place is located and also neighboring addresses.

You can do the same trick with URLs. As you can see from the following example, you can break most URLs you encounter into three parts, the last two of which are really interesting.

```
http://    www.nasa.gov    /mission_-
                           pages/shuttle/main/index.html
Protocol   Host            Path
```

Think of a URL's path as specifying a postal address, written from the right to the left (USA, CA, San Francisco, 5 Mulberry Ave, Ms

Jane Smith). By removing the address's elements from right to the left you can obtain coarser descriptions (the home, the street, the city, the state, or the country). The elements of a URL's path are separated by a /. Often, by removing these elements in a similar way you can reach broader areas of a web site. When you remove them all, you'll reach the web site's main page.

Thus, if through a web search you've landed on a presentation or a PDF document that does not contain any navigation options, you can navigate on your own by "hacking" the document's URL. This method doesn't always work (it depends on how the specific site is constructed), but it works often enough to be very useful.

For instance, through a web search you may land on a NASA document containing instructor notes on the photogeologic mapping of the Moon

```
http://solarsystem.nasa.gov/educ/docs/Photogeologic_
Map_Moon.pdf
```

It's difficult to find the context of that document. However, removing the last two parts of the URL will give you

```
http://solarsystem.nasa.gov/educ/
```

which is NASA's solar system exploration education page.

4.4 Locate orphan pages through link queries

If the method of hacking a URL to pieces, which we explored in item 4.3, doesn't work, an alternative is to ask Google for pages that link to that page. Typing in Google's search box the word link: followed by the page's URL will do the job. For example, a Google search for

```
link:solarsystem.nasa.gov/educ/
```

will return the six pages that link to it. Needless to say, you don't
need to retype the URL, just copy-paste it from your browser's
address bar.

4.5 Bookmark sparingly

Bookmarks on web browsers seem like a neat idea. When you
encounter an interesting page, you can set a bookmark to it (add
the page to your favorites, in the parlance of the Internet Explorer),
and thereby be able to find it again when you want it. The trouble
with this idea is that there are many more interesting pages than can
fit on your bookmark menu. Soon it will overflow, and you'll find
yourself spending valuable time to organize your bookmarks into
an elaborate system of folders. Or you'll let bookmarks accumulate
and become useless, because you'll not be able to browse through
them.

The solution to this problem is simple: don't bookmark! Create only
a dozen of bookmarks for the pages you visit daily. (If you visit
regularly more pages, how do you manage to do any work done?)
For all those other interesting pages that you encounter, resist the
temptation to bookmark them. If you need to access the page again
sometime later you can find it through your browser's history, by
typing its title or URL in the browser's navigation bar. If you want
to go back to the page many days later, you'll just type a couple
words into Google. Believe me, Google will find it more efficiently
than you'd be able to find it through your disorganized heap of
bookmarks. This practice will save you the time of bookmarking
the page (admit it: you never visit again most of the pages you
bookmark), and the time of organizing your bookmarks. More
importantly, you'll be able to access right away the few bookmarks
you actually use.

4.6 Make your bookmarks accessible

We saw earlier, that keeping more than a dozen bookmarks isn't really worth it. Given these few bookmarks are the ones you visit regularly, it makes sense to simplify this access. Spend some time giving them sweet and short, memorable names. Then organize them into a toolbar, or a favorites window that you'll keep pinned down at all times. Their short names mean that they won't occupy valuable real estate of your screen. Having them always available means that your favorite sites will always be one click away. Consider ordering them alphabetically, so that you can easily find the element you're looking for. For bookmarks with a nice icon you can also eliminate their names entirely, and recognize them just by their icon. This allows you to cram more bookmarks onto the toolbar.

4.7 Save web links with your other files

Storing your files into separate folders keeps them nicely organized and easily accessible (see item 11.2). As a bonus you can also use each folder to store links to related web pages. Simply use the mouse to drag the icon appearing on your browser at the left of the web page's URL to the corresponding file folder. A new link will be created within the folder, named after the corresponding web page. Then, you can easily open the page by double-clicking on the link.

4.8 Shorten your links

Long links to web sites don't travel well. It's difficult to spell them over the phone, email programs tend to break them into pieces, you can't fit them on a business card, and copying them from a printed document to a web browser is a nuisance. Therefore, if you have a long link you want to share, pass it through a so-called URL shortener service, such as bit.ly[1] or goo.gl,[2] and use its shortened form. These sites allow you to paste a long link into a box, and will then print a short form of it. For example, the link

```
https://en.wikipedia.org/wiki/Declaration_
of_the_Rights_of_Man_and_of_the_Citizen
```

becomes 21 characters long[3] on bit.ly and 20 characters long[4] on goo.gl.

4.9 Let your group vote

What would you like to do in your next team building activity? How can our children's school be improved? What would you ask our CEO who'll visit the office next week? As a group you can answer these and countless other questions, by fielding suggestions ("Let's spend a day at the beach"), discussing them ("I don't think Jenny, who's eight months pregnant, would appreciate skydiving as our team activity"), and, finally, voting among them.

You can easily do this online through Google moderator.[5] Click on *Create Series*, click on *Advanced* to select the format of the discussion, and send the link that will be created to your group. Those with the link will be able to see existing suggestions, comment on them, and vote them up or down. Hopefully some nifty ideas and winners will soon emerge.

---

[1] https://bitly.com/
[2] http://goo.gl/
[3] http://bit.ly/19VU1lC
[4] http://goo.gl/U6Flxq
[5] http://www.google.com/moderator

5. Handling Email

5.1 Read email once a day

Unless you're commanding troops in a battle by email, resist the temptation to check your email every ten minutes. Sending out replies begets more email messages, and this increases your workload.

Try to check email once or, at most, twice a day. First thing in the morning and at the close of business, should be enough. You'll see that the volume of email you're handling will decrease. Does this mean you're achieving fewer things? Certainly not; don't mistake activity for accomplishment! You simply let the passage of time trim out the essential messages from the frivolous ones. Perhaps that email soliciting ideas for the office's Christmas party by noon wasn't so important after all. You also educate your correspondents not to send you a message every time your name crosses their mind. Perhaps your colleague who wanted to join you for lunch will simply pop by your office at lunchtime, instead of organizing the expedition by email.

And if you're indeed commanding real battles by email, do your troops a favor and consider another job.

5.2 Turn-off email alerts

Email alerts, those cute balloon tips appearing on your screen to inform you that another email message is seeking your attention, are for people who think that the attention deficit disorder is a virtue.

Actually, the cost of these email notification interruptions is appalling. In 1975, the noted psychologist and tong-twister Mihály Csíkszentmihályi established the importance of a mental state called *flow*: the absorbed involvement in a challenging yet fulfilling activity. When we're in such a state we use our skills to the outmost degree; we can concentrate deeply, loosing the sense of self-consciousness and time. It can take us more than 15 minutes to enter into such a state of focused attention, and only a trivial interruption ("your imap server has 1 new message") to exit from it.

So turn off email notifications. They're not cute, and, as we saw, their cost is not just the time it takes to scan the mail's sender. And while you're at it, turn off other similar alerts, such as the notification that a friend is now online on Skype.

5.3 File incoming email

If you get more than a couple of email messages addressed to you every day, you should file your messages into folders. Just as you organize your documents into separate folders (for instance, one for each project you're involved in), so you should do for your mail messages. Ideally, create such folders with a structure similar to that of your document folders. After handling each incoming message, file it to the respective email folder. This will allow you in the future to look at the flow of communication associated with the corresponding project by browsing that folder, instead of going through thousands of irrelevant messages.

In addition, folders are useful, because there are many messages that the search facility of your email program will fail to locate. Again, having the messages neatly sorted into folders will give you a fighting chance of locating a message by sorting them in a way that matches the messages you're looking for (see item 5.19). Finally, having all messages of a project together will allow you to answer questions like the following.

- When did we start working on project Jupiter? (Order the messages by date, and look at the date of the first messages.)
- Who participated in project Mars? (Order the messages by the sender, and browse through the names.)
- How many messages did we exchange while working on project Venus? (Look at the folder's message count, and weep.)

(In most email programs you can sort a folder's messages according to a specific field, by clicking on the column's heading. A second click will reverse the sort order.)

5.4 File incoming email as you read it

For those of us who receive a moderate inflow of email messages handling our incoming email can take more than an hour a day. Often we quickly scan the email messages to see what's urgent and let the rest pile up for later handling. A more productive approach involves handling each email message that requires little of your time (say writing a one-line reply, filing it, or deleting it) as you read it. As the time you spend on those messages is minimal, this approach doesn't mess with your time management priorities, but still saves you the effort of having to read those messages a second time later on.

5.5 Don't file all incoming email

Correctly filing all incoming email, as part of the so-called "inbox zero" strategy (see item 5.4), can take up valuable time and is not always useful. Do you really need to file appropriately the heated discussion regarding your organization's yearly retreat? Instead, as part of your email handling, mark or file all important messages and then delete the rest. If you can't bring yourself to press the delete key, simply archive them in one go into a single folder.

5.6 Don't file outgoing email

Sure, go ahead and file the messages you send, if you've got plenty of free time. Otherwise, just let them accumulate in the sent items folder. The folder will, inevitably, grow large and unwieldy over time, but this is not a problem in practice, because, as you'll see, there are alternative ways for locating sent messages in it.

Most of the mail you send is replies to email that you've received and, eventually, filed away. (Unless, that is, you're working for one of those online pharmacies that keep pestering me with email messages every day.) Moreover, for email messages that you sent out without replying to another message, there will often be a reply that you've correctly filed. Therefore, the (correctly filed) email messages you've received can in most cases guide you to the (unfilled) messages you sent. Once you've found the received email message in its folder you know the outgoing message's recipient, subject, and approximate date. From those elements you can easily find the message you sent.

Once you've found that message, file it correctly. Chances are that you may need to refer to it again.

5.7 Create subfolders

When the list of your email folders can't fit on the screen it's time to split them. For instance, if you work for Acme Inc. and also run your own consulting business, you might create a folder tree like the following:

- Acme
    - Finance
    - HumanResources
    - Meetings
    - JupiterProject

  – VenusProject
- Consulting
  – OneClient
  – AnotherClient
  – YetAnotherClient
  – Prospects
- Personal
  – Friends
  – Relatives
  – Home
  – Rockclimbing
  – Sailing
  – Vacation

To keep this folder tree reasonably small you might want to create another folder named "Old", and move there folders that are not current anymore.

5.8 Create shortcut-accessible folders

Filing email messages by dragging them to their individual folders can put significant stress on your carpal joints. This happens, because you are forced to move the mouse while your hand's muscles are tensioned to hold down the mouse's button. Performing this task hundreds of times each day can be really hurtful.

You can avoid this problem by naming your subfolders so that as many as possible start with a different letter or digit. For instance, instead of having folders named "Friends" and "Family", name them "Friends" and "Relatives". This will allow you to specify each folder by typing its first letter as a keyboard shortcut. You can thus swiftly and painlessly file email messages without touching a mouse (see also item 18.4). When you've selected the message you want to file, press your keyboard's context menu button, use the keyboard to specify whether you want to move or copy the message, and navigate to the folder you want to place it using the folder's keyboard shortcut.

5.9 File to multiple folders

Sometimes you receive a mail message that could be filed to multiple folders. Where do you file it? The answer is simple: to all folders you would expect to find it.

For instance, if an email contains a status update on project Jupiter and ends with news about the birth of your colleague's daughter, you'll file it in the folders "Jupiter" and "Personal". Email programs provide commands to *copy* or *move* a message to a folder. In our example, you'll first *copy* the message to the "Jupiter" folder, and then *move* it to the "Personal" folder, so as to get it out of your Inbox.

5.10 Link folders with placeholder messages

Say you've moved a large number of messages from one email folder to a new one. How can you make a note that those messages are now in that other folder? Simple: send yourself a small email message with a descriptive subject line indicating the fact, and file it in the original folder. Here is an example.

```
Subject: MOVED: Titan messages

All messages regarding Titan's exploration
have been moved from the Saturn folder to
the Titan folder.
```

You can also follow the same trick, if you often find yourself searching for messages in a wrong folder. Add in that folder an email message pointing to the correct folder for that material.

5.11 Automate filing

Arrange for low priority email to be automatically filed. This will keep your inbox clean for the important stuff that you must act upon. You can do this by employing what mail programs call *message rules* or *filters*. In them you specify actions for messages that satisfy some characteristics. For instance, messages containing "news.economist.com" in their "From" field should go to the "Read-Later" folder, while messages containing "Make money at home" in their "Subject" field should be deleted. This technique is especially important if you subscribe to mailing lists that send out tens of messages every day. By filing their messages in a separate folder you avoid the inevitable distraction of these messages to your email-processing routine.

5.12 Don't read spam

Spam is this unsolicited email we all seem to get about pharma-ceutical remedies, cheap luxury watches, get-rich-quick schemes, hot stock tips, lonely girls looking for friendship, and lawyers of deceased dictators looking for a trustworthy person to funnel their funds to. It seems that spammers are consistently at least half a step ahead of those spam filters that are supposed to detect and delete their messages. As a result many of us are bombarded daily with spam emails.

The response to this deluge of trash is simple: don't let it disturb you. If a message's subject is suspicious and if you don't know the sender, simply press the delete button, without bothering to read the message's content. Now if `Hhjkk <buynet4u03@yahoo.mm>` really had something important to tell you in the email with the subject ' Dear sir/Madam', he'll just have to send you another notification if you delete his first email.

5.13 Don't fall for hoaxes

Every so often a well-meaning friend will forward you an email detailing the great danger of a specific virus-carrying email message, an urgent Microsoft security bulletin, advice to enter your PIN on an ATM in reverse order to signal you're under duress, the health risks of mobile phones and microwaved food, or the sad story of a dying girl that is collecting postcards. Unfortunately all these stories are hoaxes endlessly perpetrating through the internet.

If you're busy, the easiest thing you can do with such an email is to ignore it. If you've got time to spare, copy-paste a sentence from the forwarded message into Google's search box (preferably within double quotes; see item 3.3), adding "hoax" as another search term. Chances are (this has actually never failed me) that on the top of the search results you'll get a web page explaining why the message is a hoax. Having satisfied your curiosity, you can then politely point out the page to the message's sender. (Please, not to the whole recipient list.)

Whatever you choose to do, resist the temptation to forward the email to everybody in your address book. Recipients who know better may laugh at your naïvité, more innocent ones will be undeservedly deceived.

5.14 Send reminders to yourself

If you're efficiently and diligently using TODO lists to organize your activities you may skip this entry. Otherwise, consider that you can remind yourself of a task that needs doing by sending an email to yourself. It only takes a few seconds to compose such an email, and a little while later it will appear in your inbox pestering you, until you decide you've handled it.

You can also use features of your calendar program to send yourself reminders on specific days. Finally, there's a web site[1] from which you can arrange for an email to be sent to you at an certain day in the future. If you plan to use this service to remind you of your golden wedding anniversary, make sure you don't change your email address in the meantime.

5.15 Reply to mail you sent

If you want to follow-up on an email you sent earlier—perhaps to send a reminder—the best way to do this is to reply to your original email. Locate the mail you sent in the sent mail folder, and press *Reply All*. Remove yourself from the recipients and change the actual recipient's addressing from *Cc* into *To*. This type of follow-up will ensure that the email has the correct subject, recipients, and mail thread tag.

5.16 Read the recipient lists

When you receive an email, have a look at the list of recipients, both those to which the email was directly sent, and those receiving a "carbon copy" (Cc). These lists often contain at least as valuable information, as the message body itself.

- Are you expected to act on the email? Normally not, if you're on the Cc list. (A friend had a mail filter configured to delete all messages in which he was merely copied. He told me he could not recall a single instance, where he missed something important.)

---

[1]http://futureme.org

- Is your name missing from the recipient lists? In this case you received a *blind carbon copy*. Be very careful on how you act: you should definitely *not* reply to all the message's recipients. (See item 6.6.)
- Is the sender escalating an issue? A sign that something is amiss is an increasing number of recipients as emails get exchanged.
- Is the email circulating outside your organization? In that case, be careful not to include privileged information in your answer.
- Does the email contain confidential information? Then, be very careful with where you forward it and the recipients you add to your reply.
- Is somebody missing from the recipient list? This may be a mistake, which you can correct, or it may be intentional, in which case you may have witnessed a first sign of trouble.

5.17 Detach attachments

Attachments and email don't get well along together. Mail programs often have difficulty searching in them. When you file email messages containing attachments your email folders will clog with junk, unless you start deleting complete mail messages, thus loosing useful information. (At the very least email messages provide you a record of the people you communicated with and the timeframe of that email interchange.)

The best strategy for handling email messages with attachments is to save the attachment to the file folder (not the email folder) of the corresponding project, and delete it from the mail message. This keeps your email folders lean and mean, while also keeping the attachments that came with email nicely organized. If your email program doesn't provide you with a command to detach or delete an attachment, consider switching to a program that does. The free mail client Mozilla Thunderbird[2] is a choice I'd recommend.

5.18 Don't email during holidays

With a smartphone or tablet and a hotel's (oh so reasonably priced) Wi-Fi offering we're never far from our email. This is a mixed blessing. We can keep in touch with friends and relatives, and tap to the internet for planning our holiday. However, it's very difficult to relax during your vacations if every day you're confronted a deluge of work-related email. Most of us can't resist reading work-related email during the holidays; there may be urgent matters that may need our attention, or trivial ones whose messages we might want to read and delete rather than let them pile for when we return.

Fortunately, there's a way to, at least, minimize work-related email, and this is to squelch the messages you send out. Email you send generates yet more email replies. By throttling the number of messages you send out you'll see that the volume of personal email you receive will also decrease.

If your system supports it, you can also arrange for an automatic reply that will sadistically inform your overworked correspondents that you're away in an exotic location. Even if you're in fact reading email, such messages tend to minimize the inbound traffic, and also let you relax regarding the replies you ought to send.

5.19 Use multiple mail search strategies

You try to locate an email message you exchanged a couple of years ago, and, sure enough, you can't find it among the thousands you've filed away. The trick here is to try various methods for finding it; one of them is likely to succeed.

---

[2]http://www.mozilla.com/thunderbird/

- If you remember the sender, look for the sender's name.
- If (you think) you remember the subject search for it.
- If you have a rough idea of the date, order the messages by date, and scan those around that period. If you don't remember the date, try to find it by locating other, easier to find, messages that you sent around that date.
- Search for distinct unusual words that probably appeared in the message's text.
- If you can't find an email you sent, try to locate the one you received; its date will then guide you to the outgoing email. If you can't find an email you received, try to find the one you sent.

Your mail program provides you with a helpful command for searching through various fields; for instance, in Microsoft Outlook Express this is *Edit – Find – Message in this Folder*, while in the Thunderbird mail client it's *Edit – Find – Search Messages*.

6. Email Smarts and Etiquette

6.1 Use meaningful Subject lines

An email's subject line is not really optional. Although you can omit it, or reuse the subject line of a random earlier email, which you chose to reply to, this is bad form. Many people view their overflowing incoming mail folder, only through the list of senders and subject lines. An email with an empty subject line will cause them to shift their eye to the name of the inconsiderate sender, your name.

A vague subject line ("hello from a friend", "business proposition", "your pictures") may cause your recipient to mistake your email for spam and junk it. An email with an inaccurate subject line doesn't stick out like a tar on a clean beach, but is nevertheless a source of confusion. If you care about the opinion others hold about your communication skills use concise and meaningful subject lines.

6.2 Don't begin a new subject by replying to an old email

Many people read email through *threads* of related messages. Their mail reader cleverly sorts their mail into threads by looking at the identifiers of related messages stored in each message. Therefore, when you create a new discussion by replying to an old email you can confuse the recipient's email reader, making it file your message together with those of the old discussion.

What you actually wanted to do was to reuse the recipient's address. For that, simply place your mouse over it, and right-click to copy it to the clipboard, or, better yet, add it to your address book.

6.3 Quote appropriately when replying

When replying to a message, the email program includes the message you're replying to, so that the recipient can see the context of your reply. This nicely simplifies your work, but unless you put some small additional effort, the email messages you exchange quickly degenerate into a long mess.

Follow these rules when replying to email.

Trim the included message
> Remove parts that are not needed to understand your reply. At the very least remove the opening and closing formalities and any disclaimer boilerplate. Even better, leave only the parts of the message that are related to your reply. This will make it easier for your recipient to figure out the parts of the message you address. Trimming is invaluable when you discuss an issue over an email. With appropriate trimming and placement of the replies you can read the discussion like a story.

Remove attachments
> Attachments can increase substantially the message's size, without being needed to understand the reply. Shuttling the same attachment back and forth across an email discussion puts a lot of strain to the participants using slow network connections.

Place the reply consistently
> There are two conventions for including the message you're replying to. Techies prefer to write their reply *after* the

text they're replying to. This, so-called "bottom reply", is a practical convention, because it allows you to follow the email exchange like a discussion, reading from the top to the bottom. However, such replies may seem rude to the uninitiated, because they don't naturally accommodate opening formalities (Dear John).

The alternative convention, the "top reply", is to write your text at the beginning of the message. This makes the message more difficult to decipher, especially if a number of replies have accumulated at the message's end; you have to read the story from the bottom to the top of the message. Still the convention is fine, if you're sending a single reply and not starting a discussion over email.

No matter which convention you choose, never mix a top with a bottom reply. If you're replying to an email that already has a reply in it, note the convention already used and follow it.

6.4 Check your quoted text when adding recipients

As I was writing this chapter, I got an email from a colleague who was invited to participate in a meeting taking place at 14:00. Embarrassingly, at the end of the email he received, were previously exchanged emails where the other attendees organized a separate meeting at 13:30 to organize themselves.

Don't make the same mistake. When you add recipients to an email reply, verify that the quoted text is appropriate for the extended recipient list.

6.5 Don't mix private and public distribution lists

Some email lists are private and closed. They are not openly advertised, membership is by invitation only, and people participating in
them are typically very serious about keeping the list's character
private. Therefore, never send email to such a list with copies to
people who are not members of the list. It's also considered bad
etiquette to forward emails from such lists in a way that betrays
their origin.

6.6 Don't Bcc

A blind carbon copy (Bcc) is a sneaky way to send a copy of your
email to some third parties, without having their addresses shown
to the other email's recipients. Most email programs provide this
feature, but using it is, almost always, a bad idea. You'd address
somebody through a Bcc when you want to hide this fact from the
actual email recipients. For instance, your chastise Bob, one of your
reports, and Bcc Alice, your boss, so that she knows the trouble
Bob is causing you, without having Bob realize you're badmouthing
him.

This scheme can easily backfire creating you a huge embarrassment.
If Alice responds to the email through a "reply-all" command
(perhaps she didn't notice that she wasn't in the recipient list), then
her reply (and probably parts of the original quoted email) will go
to Bob. Bob will realize that you deviously sent a Bcc of your email
to Alice, and you'll end up in a tight spot. If you really want Alice
to know about your problems with Bob, simply forward her the
original email you sent him. When she replies to that, the reply will
go only to you.

6.7 Arrange for replies to go where they should

You'll ask a large group of people for feedback, but you want Bob to organize the deluge of replies into a coherent summary. Asking people to send their replies to Bob won't help a lot; most people will simply click on the *Reply* button, and you'll waste time forwarding their emails to Bob. To avoid this problem, when composing the email, set the address where replies will be directed. You do this by specifying Bob's address in the so-called *Reply-To* message header.

Unfortunately, the details on how you do this vary among email programs. For example, on Thunderbird, you click on the *To* button, while on Outlook you'll find a setting through the *Options* button. To find instructions for other email programs the web is your friend.

6.8 Don't put in an email what you don't want to see in public

Emails get forwarded, replied-to, printed and left lying around, mis-filed, subpoenaed, spied on, or published by unscrupulous crackers. When you write an email, always keep in mind that this email might one day be made public, or end up with the person you'd least want to find about it. Executives from organizations ranging from the White House to the Whitehall, from Enron to Morgan Stanley, and from Microsoft to MediaDefender have been hit by this problem. You don't want to join them.

6.9 Flames belong to the cooler

A flame email is a message you write to let off steam when you're enraged. Mentally picturing the recipient repentantly bursting to tears when he reads your message is not uncommon. (Internet folklore has those recipients asked to don an asbestos suit before opening the email message.)

Composing such an email may be psychologically therapeutic, but sending it is another matter entirely. When you calm down, you'll regret having sent it. Therefore, compose the message, if this makes you feel good, but don't send it out. File it to a folder named "cooler" (not to the unsent messages folder, from which it may get sent by mistake). Read the message again after you've slept over it. Chances are you'll then think of better ways to deal with the matter, such as a face to face meeting, a phone call, or a polite, reasoned, and constructive response.

6.10 Sandwich critique within praise

Email is a blunt instrument, lacking the nuance we add to our physical interactions through feedback and body language. When criticizing by email it's easy to get misunderstood, hurting the recipient's feelings and poisoning a relationship. To mitigate the risk, sugar the bitter pill by starting and ending your jeremiad with some praise. Here's an example.

```
Dear Bob,

Taking the initiative to wash our car over the
weekend was great! Sadly, it seems that you forgot
to close the windows before washing it, which I
found out when I ruined my new suit by sitting on
the wet seat on Monday morning. Please be more
careful next time. Nevertheless, it was a nice
change to drive to work in a sparkling car.
```

6.11 Reread before pressing send

Do yourself and your message recipients a favor: read your completed message again before pressing the "send" button. Keep your eyes open for typos, repeated words, misspellings, abruptness, confusing structure, unsuitable terminology, and violations of this chapter's advice.

The ease with which we can fire and forget email messages makes us careless and sloppy. At best a slapdash message reflects badly on our communication skills, at worst it can fail to achieve its intended effect. Spending a few extra seconds to read what we wrote pays handsome dividends.

6.12 Write short messages as a Subject line

Some messages are so short that you can write their entire content in the message's Subject. Ending the Subject with the characters "EOM" (end of message) tells the message's readers that they don't need to open the message, because there's nothing more in it. This considerate gesture will save them time, especially if they're reading your message on a mobile device. Here is an example of such a message that you might send to your colleagues.

```
Subject: Flat tire; arriving at 11:30 EOM
```

6.13 Save time with VSRE

VSRE stands for ""very short reply expected". According to the corresponding web site,[1] it's a way for you to indicate to your email's recipients that they have to reply with a short (usually one

---

[1]http://vsre.info/

to five words) message, such as "Yes", "No", "Tuesday", or "Pls send more info". Put it at the end of your message to save them the time they would spend to write an elaborate polite reply, and also save yourself the time you would need to read it.

6.14 Send mass email through a Bcc

There's one situation where an email sent through a Bcc (see item 6.6) can be the preferable option. When you're addressing an email, say a dinner invitation, to many people it's often better to send it by adding each recipient email address as a Bcc. This avoids disclosing to all other recipients, the emails of people who prefer to keep theirs private. More importantly, when, inevitably, your aunt Mabel mistakenly issues a "reply-all" command to tell you that she won't be able to attend your dinner, because her Chihuahua is suffering from diarrhea, her reply won't go to all your other guests.

6.15 Use read receipts with care

An email you compose with read receipt option (*Tools – Request Read Receipt* in Outlook Express; *Options – Deliver Status Notification* in Thunderbird) will prompt its recipients to send you back a receipt once they open your message. The utility of this receipt is a lot less than what you may imagine. A recipient may choose to ignore the prompt, and, despite its name, it doesn't actually prove that the recipient read the message, all it shows is that somebody opened it. Read receipts are also intrusive.

Therefore, don't ask for a read receipt for all your messages. A friend regularly sends me jokes by email; with a read receipt option. I haven't complained, because the jokes are really funny, but I still find the prompt obnoxious.

You can use a read receipt to signal that you consider an email particularly important. However, this signal can be effective only if you rarely use this option.

6.16 Avoid attachments

Attachments are a pain when you receive them (see item 5.17). Don't be part of the problem by sending them out. There are few more distressing things than an email message containing a plain-text Word document as an attachment. At the very least, the recipient has to click a couple more times to read it. Worse, reading this message on a mobile device can be tricky, so is filing it, or searching in it. Also, the recipient may lack the program needed to read the attachment and the permission to install it. (Large organizations are often very picky on what programs can be installed on a computer.) Therefore, never put in an attachment what you can express as plain text in a message's body.

6.17 Share large files using cloud-based services

Large files and email don't get along together. Many programs that transfer email will choke on them. Filing messages containing large attachments will make your email reading program slower. Also, a collaboration that involves emailing back-and-forth a document is tedious and error prone.

To share large files with friends or colleagues consider using a cloud-based service, such as Google Drive[2] or Dropbox[3] for documents, Flickr[4] for photos, and YouTube[5] for videos. These services allow you to upload a file to the computers of the company providing the service. These operate in a huge far-away data center

---

[2]http://drive.google.com
[3]https://www.dropbox.com/
[4]http://www.flickr.com/
[5]http://www.youtube.com/

(hence the "cloud" name). Once you upload the file, you can get a web link to it, which you can easily share by email. With suitable settings you can limit the people who can view (or even edit) a file.

Keep in mind that, although these services are generally reasonably careful with how they handle your files, when you upload a file to a cloud-based service, you give up some control over the document's confidentiality. See item 13.8 for more information.

6.18 Don't plan meetings over email

It's a huge waste of time. You email five people to setup a meeting for Monday or Tuesday 9am, and the replies (to all) start coming in. "Yes, I can make it on both days, but on Monday I have to leave at 9:30." "Sorry, I can't make on Tuesday." "I can only make it on Monday, but after 10am." "I can't make it on either day; how about Wednesday afternoon?" "Yes, Wednesday would suit me better as well." "Sorry, I have a dentist appointment on Wednesday."

Here is the productive way to do it. Go to the Doodle web site,[6] select a large set of possible days and times for the meeting, and email all potential participants the link for scheduling the event. Then everyone can visit the link to select the slots they're available. When all participants have indicated their availability (you may have to send them a reminder), choose the slot where all (or most) participants are available, and notify them. That's it!

If the organization you work for has adopted a common calendar software, then use that instead. Some calendar software features, such as Microsoft Outlook's Scheduling Assistant, offer functionality similar to Doodle for setting up meetings. Alternatively, look at each participant's calendar to find a time where all are available. In some organizations it's even acceptable to enter the meeting in the participants' calendar, saving them the time to acknowledge their participation.

---

[6]http://doodle.com/

6.19 Don't edit documents over email

Sending out a document over email to elicit comments and changes from multiple recipients can end in a nightmare when you have to consolidate the (sometimes conflicting) changes that will come back to you. Instead, store the document on a cloud-based drive (see item 6.17), provide access to the people you want to edit it, and email them the link.

When you share the document through Dropbox your collaborators can edit it with the same software you used (such as Microsoft Word or Excel), but multiple simultaneous edits will still conflict and cause trouble. Therefore this approach is OK only with a few participants who can coordinate the times they edit over email or phone. ("Friends, Jane will work on it overnight, then Andrew will take over in the morning.")

On the other hand, if you create (or upload) the file as a Google Document, then many of you can work on it simultaneously. Each one can see all others' changes, and you can even discuss the edits over phone or chat at the time you perform them.

6.20 Introduce people

John tells you he's looking for a widget specialist, and you happen to know Mary who's indeed one. You can email Mary describing John's problem, and then forward Mary's reply to John. And then you can continue wasting your time copying John's reply to Mary and Mary's to John, till death do them part.

Alternatively, simply send out an email, addressed to both, that introduces one to the other, and asks them to continue their exchange keeping you (or not keeping you) in the loop.

6.21 DON'T YELL

You may be writing email messages in all-uppercase letters, because you think email resembles the telegraph system of yore. Or maybe the application you typically use requires you to work with the "Caps Lock" key activated. None of the two reasons (or any other) is a valid excuse to write emails using uppercase characters. Many consider emails written in this style to be the written equivalent of yelling. Such text is also more difficult to read (see item 10.7). So, don't do it.

7. Working with Documents

7.1 Bookmark with undo

While working on a document, say you move up a couple of pages to see the title of a previous section. Or your hand accidentally presses Page Down, and you find yourself in a random document location. Or you run a search command to locate the spelling of a tricky name. How do you return to the place in the document where you were working on?

The answer is a remarkably powerful yet simple trick. Undo your last change, and then redo it. This will return your document and your cursor to the exact place that you were editing. If you use the corresponding keyboard shortcuts (*Ctrl-Z* followed by *Ctrl-Y* on Windows and Linux; *Cmd-Z* followed by *Cmd-Y* on a Mac), the last location you were editing is never more than three keystrokes away.

7.2 Outline

With a word processor you can see a document as both a forest and as trees. Though most of the time we look at the trees of our document—paragraphs or, at most, pages—a single command (*View – Outline*) allows us to see our document as a forest: its composition through sections and subsections (and subsubsections and subsubsubsections, if you're a member of the legal profession).

Provided you've used styles for marking the headers you're using (as level-1 or level-2 headers; see item 7.7), you'll be able to click on a header to hide or show the subsections and text lying underneath it. With a mouse you'll also be able to drag complete sections around and promote and demote section headings, reorganizing your document on the fly. In fact, outlining is so nifty, that many compose the entire document in outline view, taking advantage of the discipline it imposes to organize their thoughts.

7.3 Beware of the changes you track

Change tracking can reveal more than you want to. Often a released document turns out to contain embarrassing details of previous versions in it, for instance a lower price you rounded up, or strong words that you toned down. So, before sending-off the final version of your document make sure you've accepted all changes, and that no changes remain visible. And if you want to be really sure that your document is released swanky-clean, convert it into PDF, following the instructions[1] laid out by the experts, the US National Security Agency.

7.4 Don't align with whitespace

It's tempting to align the words on a page with the spacebar. You tap it until the words fall into place. Yet, the end result is shaky. As soon as you change the font, its size, or even add a letter, the placement crumbles into disorder like a fallen house of cards.

The correct approach is to instruct your word processor on the exact result you want to achieve. Specify explicitly the alignment as left, right or center, and your words will always appear in the correct place. Setup the paragraph indentation and the handling of the paragraph's first line, and your paragraphs will match like toys coming out of a production line. If your requirements are more sophisticated use a table to organize your words into neatly drawn columns.

---

[1]http://www.nsa.gov/ia/_files/support/I733-028R-2008.pdf

7.5 Paragraph breaks aren't for vertical spacing

The only legitimate use of pressing the "Enter" key in your document is to specify the end of a paragraph or heading. To add vertical space between paragraphs and headings use the *Spacing – Before* and *Spacing – After* properties from the paragraph's dialog box, *Indents and Spacing* tab; for table elements use the table row's height property. Taking the lazy route and adding blank paragraphs to create vertical space will make formatting adjustments a nightmare once you change a font or page style.

7.6 Break pages declaratively

Inserting a so-called "page break" in your document is in most cases a bad idea. The reason you typically do it, is because you want the text following the page break to start on a new page. However, as you edit your document you can reach a point where the text before the page break will fit in exactly one page. Then the page break will appear on the next page, which, because of it, will end up being blank.

The correct approach is to declare what you want to do. Place your cursor on the element you want to appear on a new page (e.g. a section heading), and specify exactly that through the options on the *Paragraph* dialog box, *Line and Page Breaks* tab. Even better, you can use the same approach to modify the document's template, specifying that specific elements (for instance level-1 headings; see item 7.7) should always start on a new page.

7.7 Employ styles

You can easily recognize power users of word processing programs (and even the documents they create), because they employ styles.

Styles allow you to specify *what* some text is, instead of formatting it to look that way. For instance, instead of making a section heading bold, you specify that the corresponding text should be set as "Heading 1". The word processing program then knows how to format such headings.

There are several ways to specify a style. One way involves clicking the style you want on the *Home* tab of the Microsoft Word ribbon bar. You can also use shortcuts (see item 7.19), or specify styles on the document's outline view (see item 7.2).

Once you start using styles many things become easier. You can edit the structure of your document in the outline view, you can generate a table of contents (see item 7.10), and you can also change the look of your document without having to cumbersomely change each element. Simply specify the look of each style. Even better, many publishers and organizations, supply professionally-designed templates that allow you to effortlessly follow their house style (see item 10.9).

7.8 Utilize references

Delegating the handling of cross-references in a document to your word processor means that you never need to update them when elements get renumbered. For instance, the Microsoft Word command *Insert – Cross-reference* allows you to refer to headings, figures, tables, and numbered items. You can thus insert anywhere in your document the number of an item, its actual text, or the page it appears on. Then, what you've inserted will stay current and correct throughout the lifetime of your document.

It's true that inserting a reference to section 5.12 is more tricky than directly typing 5.12 in your text. However, by the time section 5.12 becomes section 7.15 you'll be glad that these references are handled "automagically".

7.9 Use the thesaurus

Don't settle for a mediocre word, when a more powerful one is just a thesaurus click away (*Review – Thesaurus*). Explore related words, until you come up with the one that exactly expresses your thought. Often you'll discover the word on your own, while browsing the thesaurus's suggestions.

You can also use the thesaurus to find that proverbial word that's always at the tip of your tongue, but never at your fingertips doing the typing. Simply lookup in the thesaurus the first related word you can come up with.

7.10 Automate the table of contents generation

Here's another thing that the word processor will do for you. If you've used styles for specifying your section headings (see item 7.7), then creating the document's table of contents is just a matter of a few mouse clicks: *References – Table of Contents – Insert Table of contents*.

7.11 Automatically convert between upper and lowercase

Changing the case of phrase is a task a computer ought to be able to handle, and indeed it can. Simply select the phrase and click on the *Change Case* icon on the *Home – Font* ribbon tab. However, if (despite the warnings in item 10.7) you want to set some text in capital letters, it's better to specify that as a format option (*Home – Font – Font Dialog – Small caps* or *Home – Font – Font Dialog – All caps*), because this doesn't require you to enter uppercase letters when you edit the text in the future.

7.12 Paste as unformatted text

With so much information located on email messages, presentations, web pages, and spreadsheets, you often copy-paste it across
to the document you're editing. The problem is that each medium
has its own formatting style, and when you paste the text in your
document it carries that style with it. In the end, your document
becomes a mess.

The solution to this problem is easy: the *Home – Clipboard – Paste –
Paste Special* command. Through it you can specify that you want to
paste your data as "unformatted text". This removes all formatting
from the text before placing it to your document; the pasted text
inherits your document's style. You may end-up having to redo
some formatting that you actually wanted to copy—for instance
superscripts, bullets, or italic text. However, this is a lot easier than
the hassle of removing gratuitous formatting from your document.

7.13 Search and replace formatting

Did you know that your word processor's search and replace command, can also work for formatting? For instance, you can search
for underlined text (a no-no in typographic quality documents)
and replace it with italics. The functionality is neatly hidden a few
mouse clicks away: *Home – Editing – Replace – More – Format*.
Using this command, is a lot faster and more reliable than doing
those replacements by hand. The ideal is of course to use styles (see
item 7.7), instead of explicit formatting commands.

7.14 Search all word forms

Sometimes you to want to find all the forms of a specific word.
Checking the option *Home – Editing – Find – Find all word forms*
will do exactly that. For instance, if you specify "ring", Word will

also locate "rang" and "rung" You can even provide a replacement pattern, "surround", for instance, and Word will helpfully replace "ring" with "surround", and suggest "surrounded", "surrounding", and "surrounds" as possible replacements for "rung". Isn't English a wonderful language?

7.15 Search with wildcards

If you want to search like a pro, the name of the game is wildcards. Enabling the option *Home – Editing – Find – Use wildcards* will give to various characters in the text you search for a magic meaning, allowing you to generalize your search. For instance, the magic symbol * will match an arbitrary number of characters. Thus, is you're a chemist searching in your document for instances of *polyethylene, polypropylene, polybutadiene,* or *polyacetylene* you can specify as the search word `poly*ene`, and this will match any of the four compounds.

The search words using wildcards can get a lot more complex. To search for four-digit numbers (such as years), you would enter `<[0-9]{4}>`, which means search for whole words (these are delimited by the < and > pairs), containing a digit (the characters [0-9]), repeated four times ({4}). There are many more magic characters; refer to the corresponding help page, if in wildcards you've found your life's true calling.

7.16 Search for special elements

If what you're looking for is not standard text, but something such as a footnote mark, a page break, a graphic, then the button *Home – Editing – Find – Special* will enter into the search box a special code that will identify that item and search for it.

7.17 Track changes

When you collaborate with a colleague over a document it's often nice to know what changes each makes to it. Browsing 100 pages of the 15th version of the document to find a couple of changed words can be a nightmare. Fortunately, your word processor can simplify this task for you. Through the command sequence *Review – Track Changes – Track changes* you can specify that all your changes will be marked on the document through colored text and change marks. You can also specify whether you want to see those changes, or you want them to remain hidden. In the latter case, your collaborating colleagues will probably want to unhide them so that they can see what you've changed.

When you send a document off to somebody else for further processing, you can enable this tracking, so that you can then see the changes made when the document returns back to you. Furthermore, even if you both forget to track changes, there's a way out, provided you have the original version of the document at hand (see item 2.8). The *Review – Compare – Compare* command will allow you to see the changes between two documents you specify.

7.18 Avoid embedded elements and links

True, you can paste into your document a spreadsheet, a chart, or a drawing, and you can also link another document. This type of linking or embedding will update the document whenever the corresponding element changes. Yet the risks you take are greater than the convenience. First, transferring such documents is error-prone, because the recipient must often exactly match your environment (program versions and installed add-ins). Also, you may be revealing more than you intend; for instance the spreadsheet figures you used to derive the worksheet you embedded. Therefore, prefer simple pasting (through the *Home – Clipboard – Paste – Paste Special* command) to linking or embedding.

7.19 Useful shortcuts

A trait distinguishing a novice from an experienced user of an application is that the latter one will often tap a clever keyboard shortcut, instead of laboriously navigating through menus and icons with the mouse. Here are some shortcuts that are particularly useful in Microsoft Word. (If you're using a MacBook, you must press the *fn* key to use a function key, for instance *Fn-F7*.)

Copy-paste format
> *Ctrl-Shift-C* (*Cmd-Shift-C* on a Mac) will copy the formatting from the area you've selected to the clipboard. You can then select another area of text and type *Ctrl-Shift-V* (*Cmd-Shift-F* on a Mac) to make that area follow the same format as the one you copied it from. This sequence is particularly useful if the format you want to transfer from one area to the other is difficult to apply—say, a different font in bold and a slightly smaller size.

Find *Ctrl-F* (*Cmd-F* on a Mac) will open the find window, allowing you to quickly locate a word or phrase in your document. When specifying what you want to find, save your effort, typing only the fewest characters that can uniquely locate what you're looking for.

Repeat last find
> With *Ctrl-Shift-Y* (*Cmd-Shift-F4* on a Mac) you can search to find the next occurrence of the last element you located.

Spell check
> *F7* will spell-check the word you've selected.

Thesaurus

Shift-F7 will open the Word's thesaurus for the word under your cursor.

Goto

Ctrl-G (*F5* on a Mac) will allow you to jump to the page number you specify. Invaluable, when you're entering a few corrections in a long document.

Headings

Ctrl-Shift-1 (*Cmd-Option-1* on a Mac) will transform the paragraph you're on into a level-1 heading. Using the number 2 will create a level-2 heading, and so on.

8. Working with Spreadsheets

If you've never encountered a spreadsheet in your life, you're a member of an exceedingly small group of lucky people. A spreadsheet allows you to organize your numbers into a grid of rows and columns and perform calculations on them. As you can imagine, spreadsheets are rarely used for fun. Nevertheless, it won't hurt you to try one out. If you have Microsoft Office installed on your computer, start Excel to see a spreadsheet in action. You can also use Google's free web-based spreadsheet[1] without installing anything on your computer.

8.1 Replace your calculator with the spreadsheet

Whenever you're about to use a calculator for something more complex than a single arithmetic operation open-up a spreadsheet, and perform the calculation there. This has a number of advantages:

- You can review and correct the numbers you type
- You can experiment with different ways to obtain your result
- You can save the spreadsheet and use it again in the future
- The spreadsheet documents not only the result (the calculator will also do that), but also how you derived it

---

[1]http://drive.google.com/

8.2 Use multiple worksheets

There's a case to be made for keeping all the parts that make up a calculation on the same worksheet. This organization provides a bird's eye view that's also easy to navigate. However, when the calculation becomes too complex, or when you're storing on the same spreadsheet various unrelated data sets, then it's time to use those tabs at the bottom, and split your cells into multiple worksheets.

Have the first sheet contain your input and output data (or a summary), and devote separate worksheets to the nitty-gritty calculations. Add as many worksheets as you need. If you're already using each sheet's two dimensions you can use multiple worksheets with the same structure to establish a third dimension for your data. Give each worksheet a meaningful name (right-click on the name); the default names Sheet1, Sheet2, and Sheet3 aren't going to help you locate what you're looking for in a couple of months' time. Finally, if you send such a spreadsheet to a non-expert it might be helpful to point out that it contains multiple worksheets.

8.3 Structure your spreadsheet for calculations

The road to hell is paved with good intentions. There are infinite unproductive ways to tart up your spreadsheet. For example, you can add multiple header rows, you can merge some of the header columns together, or you can add subtotals and subheadings within a long list of numbers. All these actions may indeed make your spreadsheet look prettier, but they will also make it far less usable. Multiple header rows will confuse sorting operations, merged cells will hinder copy-pasting, and subtotals will break functions that work on ranges.

Therefore, follow the KISS (keep it simple, stupid) principle, and avoid adding fancy adornments to your spreadsheet. Use a single header row and have each column devoted to exactly one type of values. For instance, put all of a model's sales figures in column D: avoid scattering sales figures for the same model into a column for each year, and refrain from putting in the same column quarterly sub-totals.

If you actually want to (or must) present your results in a fancy way, do the following. Create a separate "presentation' worksheet that pulls the figures from your simple but powerful "calculation' sheet. In the "presentation' sheet go wild adding all the bells and whistles (and pink unicorns) you want.

8.4 Name your data

It's easy to get carried away with the power of the spreadsheet, and create elaborate schemes of cells that get calculated from other cells. The problem is that worksheets created in this way can quickly become inscrutable. You can make your formulas a lot more readable if you assign names to cells (or cell ranges), and then you refer to those cells by their name; the corresponding buttons lie in the *Formulas – Defined Names* ribbon section. For instance, instead of having a cell contain the formula =H19*F17, you can name H19 as Final_Price and F17 as Euro_Rate, and then write the formula as = Final_Price * Euro_Rate.

8.5 Keep an extra row

Here's a potentially expensive mistake. When you add an extra item by inserting a row exactly above a sum formula the sum won't include the value of that row. To avoid this problem, note that when you insert a row in a spreadsheet it gets inserted above the row you're located, and the area ending at that row expands to encompass that new row. Thus, sums and similar functions over that new area will compute the correct result.

In order to always be able to add the row within the area you're interested in, make it a habit to leave one empty row (or column) at the end of your data, and put the formulas computing values over the area *after* that row. The area that these formulas work on should include that row. When you want to add an extra row, add it *above* the empty row. The area in the formulas will then be correctly updated.

For instance, if you want to sum the sales figures of 10 dealerships, put the values in rows 1–10, leave row 11 empty, and put the sum function in row 12 as SUM(1:11). When you want to add another dealership, add it above row 11. The formula will be correctly updated into SUM(1:12). In this way you can add as many dealerships as your company can afford, and the formula will stay correct.

In contrast, if you add a row exactly above a formula, that row will not get included in their area, and the results will be wrong. In our example, the formula will stay as SUM(1:10), even after you add a dealership in row 11.

8.6 Don't show numbers with meaningless precision

A chart or table showing the weekly sales percentages corresponding to each car model for 15 cars with a precision of two decimal places is ridiculous. A two-digit number went into the calculation, therefore a result displaying more than two significant figures falsely represents an unwarranted precision. It is also less comprehensible. In our example, if a model sold 7 units, you should display its percentage as 47%, not as 46.67%. Therefore, in this case you should change the format of the cell setting the number of decimal places to zero.

8.7 Apply formatting to whole rows and columns

When you apply formatting to a range don't constrain the format to the area covered by your data. Select the whole row or column (by clicking on the corresponding row or column label, e.g. C or 15) and apply the format there. Sooner or later you'll add more data, why not have it appear with the correct format?

8.8 Auto-complete your labels

If your labels consist of numbers, months, weeks of the day, or repetitive sequences, you can effortlessly fill long ranges with them. Simply type the first two or three, select them, and then drag down the mouse extending the area you want to fill. For instance, extending January and February will provide you the names of all months, while extending the sequence 1, 4, 7 will give you 10, 13, 16, 19, 22. (If you ever find the sequence in the last example useful, I'd be interested to know.)

8.9 Average by selecting

You have tons of numbers, and want to see the average value of a particular range. There's no need to enter a formula in your spreadsheet. Simply select the range with the mouse or keyboard, and look at the spreadsheet's status line at the bottom of the program's window. There you'll see the average, the count, and the sum of the numbers you selected. Right click on the status bar and you can enable the display of additional values that might interest you, such as the minimum and the maximum value of the selected range.

8.10 Have others fill-in your spreadsheets

Through Google's cloud-based spreadsheet you can easily create a web form that others can use to enter data into your spreadsheet. The four steps you need to follow are the following.

- Go to Google Drive,[2] and sign-up, if you haven't ever done so
- Click on *Create – Form*
- Edit the form, specifying its fields
- Send an invitation to those you want to fill the form for you

By specifying on the form that a field can get only some fixed values, you can ensure that your spreadsheet will only contain valid data. The data entered on the form will appear on your Google drive as a spreadsheet. If you want to process it with Excel you can download it using the command *File – Download as – Microsoft Excel.*

---

[2]http://drive.google.com/

9. Preparing and Delivering Presentations

9.1 Plan two minutes per slide

The Harvard Law School professor Lawrence Lessig has a unique presentation style, which involves going through his slides at a rate that often amounts to a slide per word. However, most of us work through our presentations at a rate of approximately two minutes per slide. Unless you've actually timed yourself, never assume you can do better than that. Planning to cram 60 slides on a half-hour presentation is flirting with disaster. Always use the conservative estimate, but also keep an eye on your watch. Your audience will be grateful if you finish earlier, but will not forgive you if you run over your allotted time; especially if you extend your presentation into the time of the coffee break.

And if Lessig gives a talk in your area, plan to attend; it's an experience not to be missed!

9.2 Skip slides when in a hurry

When you've overrun your allotted time, don't try to speak faster or to omit details from slides. Your audience will find it difficult to follow the presentation, and through your stressed behavior you'll be constantly reminding them that you've run out of time. Instead, plan in advance which slides are less important, and skip them advancing toward the presentation's conclusions.

9.3 Avoid running text

You may have copied to your presentation some text from a web page or white paper to save writing effort. Or, you may have written on your slide a long-winded sentence, because (according to Blaise Pascal) you lacked the time to make it shorter. Or, you may think that putting exactly what you want to say on your slides will save you the effort of memorizing your presentation.

None of the preceding reasons is a valid excuse for ruining your presentation. Slides with running text look awful, because they are crowded. The inevitable cramming of text with small fonts also makes them difficult to read. And they distract your audience, which, despite the small fonts, will nevertheless try to read the slides instead of following your talk. A presentation's slides are for visual material: charts, figures, pictures, and (at most) short bullet text. These elements will guide you and your audience through your talk. If you need further help, you can paste as much text as you want into the slides' "notes" section.

9.4 Use charts

Don't use a table for what you can show with a chart. A table forces your audience to read, a chart makes them think. A table obliges you to use small fonts to make it fit, a chart allows you to splash color and graphics. Tables are for careful deliberation and reporting, charts are for getting a point across. Charts are for presentations.

9.5 Add graphics

Slides consisting of bullet points are a dry, boring affair. Worse, such slides transfer by association the same qualities to your presentation. As my colleague Einar Høst put it: "Bullets kill presentations". Sprucing up the slides with graphics will make them look livelier, though a cynic might call this the "painting a dead body approach". Nevertheless, if your content is good, it will look even better, if it's bad, your audience might still remember that at least the presentation was interesting.

Adding graphics to the slides can be a fun way to spend a couple of what might otherwise be unproductive hours (see item 2.3). Either use the clip art that comes with your presentation program, or, even better, browse the web for suitable images. An efficient way to locate images is through Google's image search.[1] Keep however in mind that many images may be subject to copyright restrictions. To be on the safe side, you can search for images on sites that provide only freely licensed material, such as Wikimedia Commons,[2] or by specifying "Only search within Creative Commons-licensed content" on Flickr's advanced search page.[3] After you find a suitable image, you can move it to your presentation by right-clicking on it, selecting from the context menu the *Copy Image* function, and then pasting it to your presentation.

9.6 Use full-screen images

Select high-resolution (large) images for your presentation, and scale them to be exactly or slightly larger than the slide's area. ("Bleeding" is the charming technical term for images that extend beyond the page's borders.) Many image sites allow you to select the size of the image to download. Select images sized 1024 × 768 pixels (dots), which offer a good compromise between resolution (clarity) and file size. If the image's dimensions and resolution don't allow it to fit on your slide, make the slide's background black. Full-screen images doing away with the, often jejune, title and the presentation's unsightly background add extra oomph to your presentation.

---

[1] http://images.google.com
[2] https://commons.wikimedia.org/
[3] http://www.flickr.com/search/advanced

9.7 Use appropriate fonts

Your slides should contain few words, so your aim is to use a font that's legible from a distance, rather than a font that's designed for running text. Therefore, set your slides in sans-serif fonts, such as Arial and Helvetica (see also item 10.1). If you want to experiment with another font, select one with clean outlines, thick strokes, and minimal decorative elements.

9.8 Avoid fancy layouts and effects

You've probably seen this presentation at least once. Each slide appears on a glitzy background of a flashing night scene, slides move away with astounding curtain-effect transitions, and the slide's bullet points come in one-by-one, agonizingly slow, dancing and singing. Sometimes, to the delight of everyone in the audience, eventually the presentation program crashes, taking the presenter down with it.

The problem with fancy presentations—apart from the fact that most of us lack the talent to make them appealing rather than appalling—is that the audience ends up paying attention to the extravagant animations and not to what you're trying to convey. Which is OK, if your talk is content-free (many are), or if your goal is simply to entertain your audience. Otherwise, keep your slide style clean and simple, and minimize the transition effects you use. Have your slides support your presentation, not distract from it.

9.9 Use a master style

I'm sure you've seen presentations that have on every slide a cute logo of the author's organization, or project, (or pet dog, if you work in a primary school). If you want your presentation to have a similarly fancy style, you don't need to copy-paste the logo on each one of your slides. Instead, through the command *View – Presentation Views – Slide Master*, edit what is called the master slide. This is a slide on which all your other slides are overlaid. You can add there the logo, and more, such as your name, the name of the presentation, and, for good measure, the name of your sponsor. From that slide you can also change the background and the fonts appearing on all other slides.

If in the future you decide to give your presentation another look, all you have to do is to change the master slide; unless you've applied style changes to individual slides, the other slides will automatically follow their master. Furthermore, by adopting this approach you save the effort of tailoring each slide, and you also create an, often dramatically, smaller presentation file.

9.10 Don't read your slides

Unless you're talking to kindergarten children or other people who can't read your presentation, resist the temptation to read your slides. First, you're insulting those in front of you by implying that they can't read. Second, you're boring them by narrating what they've already read. And, third, your delivery becomes hopelessly stilted. Don't repeat the bullet points, use them as roadmaps to guide you through what you've got to say. Keep this in mind when you're preparing your slides, putting on them the minimum number of words that will suffice for that purpose (see item 9.3).

If you can't afford to stray away from a pre-scripted text (say you're reporting to the world the findings of your investigation on weapons of mass destruction in a secretive country) prepare a separate document with your talk, and read it, while someone else advances through your slides.

9.11 Use both screens

If you're presenting with your laptop, chances are that you have a powerful tool at hand. You can setup the laptop so that the slide show will appear on the projector, while on your screen you'll see the outline, the current slide, and, most importantly, the slide's notes. This will allow you to see each slide's notes, without having those notes appear on the projector's screen. You can then create a presentation with less text that will be easier to follow; the audience will concentrate on your words and not on the projector screen.

To achieve this feat you need to setup the projector so that your desktop *extends* to that area, rather than appearing as a *copy* (duplicate or clone) on it. On Windows 7 and later versions, pressing *Windows-P* will allow you to switch to that configuration. On older versions you can do the same by right-clicking the mouse on your computer's desktop, and then going through the sequence *Properties – Settings – Extend my Windows desktop onto this monitor*. Many laptops also offer special software or a function key to perform this delicate operation. This setup isn't trivial, so practice it well in advance. Having extended your desktop to the projector you then need to instruct PowerPoint to display your slide show using the projector. For this follow the sequence *Slide Show – – Set Up – Set Up Slide Show – Multiple monitors – Display slide show on – Secondary monitor*. Again, practice delivering a presentation in this configuration, because it takes some time to get the hang of using two screens concurrently. However, once you try such a setup you'll never look back.

9.12 No live demos

No matter how confident you are about your presentation skills, re-sist the temptation to demonstrate live anything computer-related. No matter if what you want to show is some new software, an online service offering, or even a simple a web site, with a live demo you're flirting with disaster. Bill Gates famously ignored this when showing a pre-release version of Windows 98 at the 1998 COMDEX show. The computer he was using for the demonstration crashed with the infamous blue text screen, which Windows systems display when they encounter a serious error. The technical press had a field day. Your demo may not fail as spectacularly, but chances are that something will go wrong, because you'll be nervous, in an unfamiliar environment, and with a computer connected to various strange devices.

What can you do instead? The simplest solution is to take screen pictures (screen dumps in the industry parlance) of what you want to show. You can easily do this by pressing the *Alt-PrtSc* (*Ctrl-Shift-Cmd-3* on a Mac) keys to capture the image of the currently active window, or *PrtSc* (*Ctrl-Shift-Cmd-4* on a Mac) to capture the computer's entire screen. This will copy the screen contents to the clipboard, from which you can easily paste them into your presentation. If what you want to show involves elaborate actions, then you can purchase software that will record your interactions with the computer as a movie, which you can easily import into your presentation.

9.13 Arrange for backup equipment

Projector lamps eventually die, laptops crash, and the two often refuse to talk to each other. If your presentation is important, arrange for backup equipment to be at hand. It doesn't have to be state of the art, and it doesn't have to be on the floor. Simply know where you can call to get another projector, or who will be willing to lend you their laptop to deliver the presentation.

Of course, if your presentation is critical, you need to have hot (running) spares of everything, including power. But in that case professionals should be running the show.

9.14 Verify your setup

Unless you sell presentation equipment for a living, your audience is waiting to hear your presentation, not watch you juggle with cables and screen settings. Therefore, setup your presentation's equipment well in advance. Ensure that the slides do not appear cropped (especially if you have a slide titled "Brass fittings"). Also, if you're not using the computer on which you prepared the presentation, go through each slide and verify that it appears correctly. Pay attention to fonts, embedded files, and colors, which often tend to misbehave. Finally, if you're using a wireless microphone, make sure it's charged or that it has a fresh battery installed.

9.15 Setup accessible backups

I use a presentation's slides to guide me through its delivery. Without them I'm lost; sometimes I can't even remember the presentation's title. Therefore, being asked to talk without my slides is for me equivalent to finding myself naked in front of the audience. (Actually worse; with the naked stunt I can at least plead insanity.)

Chances are that your memory is a lot better than mine, but, nevertheless, loosing your presentation can be disastrous. For this reason arrange to be able to access copies of it. One good backup plan is to send it by email to your host. Carrying it with you on a CD or USB stick is another option (see item 15.2 on how to carry the USB stick). Finally, you can also send a copy to a web-mail account or store it on a cloud-based drive (see item 6.17) from which you can retrieve it through the internet.

10. Icing the Cake: Typography

With high-quality laser printers near every desktop, one might think that everyone can now create documents of typographical quality. In truth this quality goes only skin-deep, affecting only how pages are rendered on the printed output. Beyond the surface a layperson will sense an unprofessional look and feel, while a professional will quiver at the sins committed every day against the basic rules of typography. This chapter contains the most common faux pas; avoiding them will not make you a master of typography, but will allow you to fake one quite convincingly.

10.1 Use fonts wisely

The first time people discover the multitude of fonts available on their computer, they inevitably start experimenting, creating "ransom note" documents containing as many different fonts as they can cram on a page. This is a recipe for disaster. The many fonts on our PC are there so we can select one or at most two fonts for a given document or presentation. Using more fonts shows poor taste and a lack of experience in document design.

Everyday (not decorative) fonts come in two families: serif (such as the font used for the text in this paragraph, which have small protrusions at the end of each stem) and sans-serif (such as the font used in the Mobil and FedEx logos, which lack them). A rule of a thumb is to use serif fonts (for instance, Times) for running text and sans-serif fonts (such as Arial and Helvetica) for display text: presentations, headings, advertisements, and signs. Serif fonts are easier on the reader; the protrusions (serifs is the technical term) guide the eye from one letter to the next; you should therefore prefer them for setting lengthy texts.

Now that you know your fonts, look at how text is set around you, and notice how they're applied in practice.

10.2 Avoid table rules

Another common beginner mistake is to neatly split the cells of each table into a fence-like grid, using those handy horizontal and vertical rules. If you look at professionally-designed documents you'll see that tables are rarely laid out in this way. When professionals design tables they use few, if any, rules, typically employing them only to separate the headings from the table's data. Do the same; your tables will look cleaner, and your data will stand out.

10.3 Know your symbols

The symbols available on a standard computer keyboard are a haphazard collection drawn together mostly by accident. Some of the keyboard's characters were OK for sending telex messages (if you were born before 1970 you might remember their punched paper tapes) but, like a caveman in a cocktail party, they look decidedly out of place in a modern document. Therefore, try to use the correct symbols in your text. Some word processing programs will automatically guess the appropriate symbol and insert it in place of the plain equivalent; for instance Microsoft Word has an "autoformat" option (*Word Options – Proofing – AutoCorrect Options – AutoFormat As You Type*) to do exactly this. You can also insert the symbols explicitly using a shortcut key (see below), or you can select the symbol from a menu (*Insert – Symbol – More Symbols – Special Characters*). If a program doesn't offer a corresponding command, you can type the symbol in a program that does, and copy-paste it across. Without further ado, here are the symbols missing from your keyboard.

- The em-dash, which is used to separate parenthetical sentences—such as this one. Its name comes from its width: similar to that of the "m" character. Don't use a hyphen (-) instead.
- The en-dash, which is used to specify ranges, for instance, 1869–1948. Its name derivation is left as an exercise to the reader. Again, don't use a hyphen (-) instead.
- The opening and closing single quotes: 'quoted word'. The opening single quote is also used as an apostrophe. Don't use the straight single quote (') instead.
- The opening and closing double quotes: "quoted word". Don't use the straight double quotes (") for this.
- The ellipsis … Don't use a sequence of three dots (. . .) instead.

If you're using Microsoft Word, here are the keyboard shortcuts for entering the wider dashes, which, in contrast to the quotes and the ellipsis, Word does not recognize automatically.

Name	Symbol	Word Shortcut	Mac Shortcut
en-dash	–	*Ctrl-Numeric -*	*Opt -*
em-dash	—	*Ctrl-Alt+Numeric -*	*Opt-Shift -*

10.4 Prefer charts over tables over text

This rule is simple: don't set in words what you can lay out as a table, and don't use a table for data you can present as a chart. With word processors and spreadsheet programs both options are straightforward. By using tables and charts you'll make your text easier to follow, doing yourself and your readers a favor.

10.5 Prefer scalable formats

There are two ways in which your computer represents pictures. One involves drawing with letters and various shapes, such as lines and circles. We call such pictures with the ominous-sounding name "vector images". Another way is to color individual small rectangles (the so-called pixels), like my grandmother's needlework. These pictures are called bitmaps.

Vector images, the ones for instance you create in Microsoft Word, PowerPoint, or Visio, allow you to expand them without any loss of quality. The also tend to occupy less space. Professionals who print books and magazines love vector images, because they come out crisp and shiny on their high-quality printing machinery. On the other hand, some images, such as digital photographs and scanned pages, or those you create in a paint program, start their life as bitmaps.

What does all this mean to you? It's simple: create vector images whenever possible—avoid using a paint program when you can draw your picture in vector format. And when you have something in vector format, don't downgrade it by saving it as a bitmap.

10.6 Avoid underlined text

Underlining is used for emphasis in handwritten text and was also carried over in this capacity in typewritten documents. With modern printers and software you don't need to underline, because you can use a different font style (bold or italic) for emphasis. If you search for underlines in a professionally typeset book, you won't find any. Take this as a hint to avoid underlining in your documents.

10.7 Avoid uppercase sequences

TEXT WRITTEN IN ALL-UPPERCASE CHARACTERS IS AN EYE-SORE AND CONSIDERABLY MORE DIFFICULT TO READ THAN ITS LOWERCASE EQUIVALENT. LOWERCASE LETTERS HAVE BEEN DESIGNED FOR EASY READING, UPPERCASE WERE ORIGINALLY DESIGNED FOR EASY CHISELING ON STONE. UNLESS YOU'RE WRITING ONE OF THOSE SILLY PRODUCT DISCLAIMERS ("THIS PRODUCT WILL PROBABLY CAUSE YOUR CAR TO SPONTANEOUSLY COMBUST, BUT THIS WILL NOT BE OUR FAULT."), WHICH NOBODY READS ANYWAY, DON'T USE UPPERCASE CHARACTERS.

10.8 Don't be too clever

With all those features of modern word processing programs it's easy to get carried away, using every tool they provide. Yet, if your document will be professionally typeset you can end-up (like this book's author) being too clever by half. If the program you're using is not the same as the one used in production, typesetters are likely to scrap all those clever features you used, and only use your document's text. Formatting, headers, styles, footnotes, equations, tables, charts, lists, and page breaks are often typeset again from scratch. This means that all the effort you expended into nicely formatting your document is lost.

So, before playing typographer with your document, ask those responsible for its production if the program you're using is compatible with the one they'll employ. If it is, and you indeed want to control your document's appearance, ask them to give you what is called a "template" or "style file" (see item 7.7). Otherwise spare your efforts and simply concentrate on writing the text, leaving its styling to the professionals.

10.9 Use professional-designed styles

A style file or template provides the rules for typesetting a document. It specifies the margins, the spacing between paragraphs, the fonts for the running text and the headers, the typesetting of the captions, and much else. Creating such a file is a job for a professional document designer. Most word processing programs come with such files, and, if you ask, many production departments and publishers can provide you with one. Using such a file will give your document a professional appearance, which will closely resemble the end-results. This will allow you to format your document according to the production's rules and judge on your own the aesthetics of what you're writing. It will alert you of pages with too much text, or unfortunate page breaks, which you can then correct by judiciously adjusting what you write. However, unless you feel strongly about your document's appearance, or you enjoy this task, it's best to leave this fine tuning to the experts, concentrating instead on the content, rather than the presentation.

11. Data Management

11.1 Use meaningful file and folder names

Choosing names for your folders and files is an important task. Don't neglect it. "New Folder", "New Folder (2)", and "New Microsoft Word Document" aren't meaningful names. "Strategy", "Marketing", "Finance", "IT", "HR" are good choices for folder names. The last two may be cryptic to some, but if you can readily identify them as holding material related to information technology and human resources, they are fine for you. Examples of good file names are "sales-report-2008-Q1", and "reorganization-plan-v01".

For every file or folder, choose the shortest descriptive name you can come up with. The name should continue to be meaningful in a decade or two, so don't be too clever. Be consistent in your choices. If you've named one file "sales-report-2008-Q1", don't name another "2008-apr-expenses"; follow the same nomenclature and name it "expense-report-2008-Q2". Avoid placing non-English characters (such as ö) and spaces in filenames, because some programs may choke on them. Also, don't choose names that all start with the same word; this hinders your ability to select a file by typing the first characters of its name.

11.2 Organize your files

When a folder holds too many folders or files (say more than can fit on your screen) it's time to split it. Look at the files, and think of the best way to arrange them into various new folders. This could be by subject, by date, or by type. As with filenames, if you've already split some files in a similar folder, follow the same logic; don't invent a new one.

Keep low the number of folders you need to traverse in order to reach a file. Experts call this the depth of a hierarchy. Don't allow your folders to reach a depth of more than five to seven levels, or you'll be forever navigating folders instead of doing useful work. Five levels of depth with 20 elements in each folder allow you to organize 95 trillion elements. That should be enough for you, unless you're working for the NSA or Google.

Like a busy bookshelf, your files may require some cleanup from time to time. About once a year, examine the organization of your files. You might find that a split you thought was practical at a time, didn't work out as you intended in practice: some folders may be overly full while others are gathering dust. Or, material you frequently need is buried too deep in a folder hierarchy. Don't shy away from improving your filing structure, moving or renaming files and folders to create a more efficient arrangement. Unlike those hapless employees in organizations that are under perpetual reorganization, folders and files don't complain when they are renamed and moved around.

11.3 Sort files by date

Computer scientists have long known and exploited the fact that an item that was recently used will probably be used again. You can easily benefit from this observation by looking at your lists of files ordered by their modification date. To do that on Windows Explorer select the "Details" folder view (*View – Details*) and click on the "Date Modified" column; click one more time if the oldest file appears first. On a Mac click on the *View items as a list* icon, and then on the *Date Modified* column. Nine times out of ten the files you're interested in will be near the beginning of the list!

11.4 Link files with shortcuts

You're looking for a file, but you can't find it in the folder you expected it to be. After a lot of searching you finally locate it in another, related, folder.

You can ensure you can find this file the next time you'll be looking for it by creating an alias (shortcut) in the folder you thought the file would be, and making it point to the place where it actually resides. On the Windows Explorer copy (*Edit – Copy*) the file from the folder you found it, and paste it as a shortcut (*Edit – Paste Shortcut*) at the folder where your first looked. On the Mac Finder, select the file you're interested in, click on the *File – Make Alias* menu command, and move the generated alias to the other location you want it to appear. This will make the file to effectively coexist in both folders, but as a single copy. If you modify it in any of the folders, the changes will be reflected in both copies.

By the way, if you found the file you were looking for in an *unrelated* folder, simply move it to the folder it should really be.

12. Security

12.1 Beware of attachments

You too can create a highly destructive virus. Simply write in an email message the following.

```
Hi, this is a highly destructive virus!

Forward this message to ten of your
friends.  Then, throw your computer out
of the window.
```

This virus relies on the culpability of the email's receivers to thrive, and in the proposed form it won't get very far. However, many destructive viruses and worms use a similar approach, having you open an email attachment that will perform (without you realizing it) their sinister goal. Currently a popular malware activity is to encrypt all your files, and ask you for ransom (about $300) to decrypt them. Therefore, be extremely wary of opening attachments.

Opening an attachment on your computer is like inviting somebody in your home. Just as an indiscreet visitor will peek in your refrigerator and medicine cabinet (I have a friend who does that), similarly, an attachment can look at your address book and files. A visitor can go further, making a long-distance phone call while you're busy, or slipping a silver spoon in his pocket (no, as far as I know, I don't have such friends). Similarly, an attachment can send spam from your computer, or setup your computer as a base for attacking other computers (yes, things are currently ugly in the cyber world). Common sense dictates that you don't invite complete strangers to your home, and you don't open the door in the middle of the night without verifying the identity of the caller. Similarly, if you receive an attachment from somebody you don't know, or an attachment you don't expect from someone you know, it's best not to open it.

A particularly common form of attacks involves mail purporting to be from Microsoft, Apple, Google, or your company's "IT support department". The mail warns you about a security problem on your software setup, or a dangerous new virus, or that your computer has been compromised. It also asks you to execute an enclosed attachment to rectify the problem. Hopefully, you now realize that the attachment *is* the problem; the only sensible action with these emails is to delete them.

If you think there's a possibility that an attachment is legitimate, simply ask back for a confirmation. Malicious attachments are sent by automated programs, and these aren't programmed to respond to email. Unless somebody is targeting an attack specifically at you (in which case most of us don't stand a chance), a reply is a pretty good hint that the attachment is actually intended for you.

12.2 Don't reply to spam and malware senders

What's worse than spending time reading spam (see item 5.12) email? Replying to it. Replies to spam email or messages containing malware attachments (viruses and the like) are a waste of time. First, the sender address is likely to be faked. So if you receive an email from a friend with a virus, notifying her that she's infected (err... that her computer is infected) might just scare her without a reason, because the virus could have well plucked her email address from another mutual friend, and used it to propagate itself. In addition, in the unlikely event that an address you reply to is a spammer's real email address, your removal request will most likely fall on deaf ears. A colleague has even suggested that your request tells spammers that somebody reads their email, and thereby attracts even more spam.

12.3 Beware of phishers

Phishing (you really don't want to know the origin of this word) is a fraudulent attempt to obtain sensitive information, such as your account number or e-banking password. Phishers work by masquerading as a trustworthy entity, such as your bank, eBay, Amazon, or PayPal. Needless to say, that having obtained the information they're after, they'll scoop your accounts dry. Falling prey to a phisher can mean that somebody else will take that exotic vacation you were saving for; on your expense.

Typically, a phishing scam starts with an email: from your bank, asking you to verify your personal details, from an eBay user complaining about an expensive item you haven't delivered, or something similar. Once you'll click on the link provided in the mail message, your web browser will open a page that will look almost identical to that you'd expect to see. The page will include all the logos, legal boilerplate, and even warning messages to guard yourself against phishing attacks! However, the details you'll type on that page will end up with the criminal gang orchestrating the scheme. As the following gem shows, phishing does not necessarily have to direct you to a web site.

Your account has been temporarily
inactivated due to our general security
policy. In order for us to activate your
account, please send the following
documents:

1) A copy of all Credit Cards, both front
   and back side.
2) A copy of a valid identification document
   (passport, driver's license).
3) A copy of any utility bill (bank
   statement, electricity, insurance) with
   your name and address on it.

Please fax your documents to (888) xxx-xxxx.

We assure you that your personal data and
documents will not be transferred to third
parties.

Please note that all information which is
sent by fax has to be clearly readable,
otherwise we will need to re-request the
verification documents.

If you should require further assistance,
please contact us again as we are at your
service 24 hours a day, 7 days a week.

Thank you for using PayPal
The PayPal Team

Like all scams, the way to avoid phishing attacks is to recognize
them as such, or to conduct your affairs in a way that avoids them.

You can often recognize a phishing email by subtle differences between that mail and the one you typically receive from your bank or other party. For instance, the email may not include your full name or your account number. In less well-polished attempts, the mail may contain grammar or spelling mistakes (if the crooks could write well, they probably would be earning a fortune writing children's books, instead of attempting to defraud you). In other cases the web site you'll be redirected is obviously not the one associated with the institution that supposedly sent you the email. However, don't count on these signs for recognizing phishing scams, because attempts get better every day; I recently almost fell for one.

You can avoid phishing attacks, by never clicking on web links sent to you by email. If your bank asks you to "validate your account details" (highly unlikely, but I've sometimes seen banks, who should know better, behave like phishers), don't click on the link in the email. Instead, (carefully) type your bank's actual web site name on your web browser, verify that you've typed it correctly, and manually navigate to the place where you can perform whatever task is required.

12.4 No one will give you millions by email

You get this email or Facebook message from a deposed dictator, former minister, dying rich merchant, bank employee, or an inheritance-handling solicitor, who has a fortune stashed somewhere inconveniently, and needs your help to get his hands on it. Needless to say, that for your cooperation he's promising you a hefty percentage of those ill-gotten gains.

This is how an "advance fee" or "419" scam usually starts. (The 419 number refers to the article of the Nigerian Criminal Code dealing with fraud.) If you make the mistake to reply, the fraudster will send you official-looking documents backing his claim, and pretend to start the process for transferring the funds. At some point he'll ask you to wire him some money to oil the wheels, and then for more and more. No matter how much money you send over, you'll never get your hands on the treasure, because it's simply not there. You're being defrauded. To see how these people operate you can visit a web site[1] that showcases some hilariously unsuccessful attempts of this scam.

12.5 Don't click on all hyperlinks

A hyperlink is the technical term for a web link: those, often blue or underlined, words that you click to visit a web page. Like a black hole, you never know where a hyperlink will drive you. It can be an interesting and funny web page, or it can be a web page that will attack your computer or trick you into divulging sensitive data (see item 12.3). Some perverted computer nerds even enjoy convincing you to click on hyperlinks that open pictures so disgusting that will ruin your whole day.

Therefore, don't click on every hyperlink you see in front of you. Links on serious, trustworthy sites (see item 4.2) are OK. So are also links on emails from friends and colleagues, when accompanying message text indicates that they actually wrote that email. On the other hand, a link on a seedy web site (for instance, a site offering downloads of pirated wares) or a link in an email message with the accompanying text "check this out" can well be a trap.

12.6 Select unguessable passwords

Every day I get a security report for a computer server I manage. And every day somebody around the world will try to break into

---

[1]http://www.scamorama.com/

the computer by guessing passwords for various common account names. Such an account name could be yours. Therefore, select a password that is very difficult to guess. This means following these rules.

- The password should not be a word (password guessers try every word in the dictionary).
- The password should not even be a proper noun. I've seen password guessers try names of German politicians of the Nazi period and ancient Greek gods.
- The password should be at least nine characters long. Shorter ones are too easy to guess.
- The password should contain letters, numbers, and symbols. On older Windows systems password guessers can try all combinations of letters and digits in a few hours.

A good way to choose a strong password is to select a phrase (like this one), take the first letter of each word (`Agwtsapitsap`), and, finally, substitute some letters with similar looking or sounding digits or symbols (`A9wt$apit5ap`). Password crackers get better each year, but for the time being, these measures should be enough to keep you safe.

12.7 Don't reuse passwords

Every few months a popular web site reveals that its users' passwords became exposed. If your password was among them, and you reused that password on other sites, sinister crackers can try it automatically on those other sites and cause you grief. To prevent this from happening, you'd have to change your reused password on all sites you've used it, which can be tricky and time-consuming. Therefore, don't reuse a password, even on sites you think there's nothing to protect with it. Web sites evolve, and for some of them your password may in time become a valuable asset. Better safe than sorry.

12.8 Apply security fixes

Unbelievably, the security of your computer is part of a ferocious arms race. Security researchers and criminals search daily for ways to gain access to it through bugs in the programs you're running, while the organizations that wrote those programs rush to patch them up, before they become widely exploited. There's even an (underground) market where people who discover vulnerabilities sell them to groups that use them (including government agencies).

The good news is that you're not alone: millions of other computers participate in this race, and therefore, it's unlikely that once a vulnerability is discovered your computer will be immediately attacked. The bad news is that if you connect your computer to the internet, or exchange files and email with others, eventually you'll get attacked; criminals routinely scan every computer on the internet for weaknesses. Once they get access to a machine, they recruit it to join the million-strong armies of "zombie" computers they maintain for their nefarious purposes.

So-called firewalls—programs or devices that isolate your computer from the internet—can somewhat mitigate the threat of these attacks. However, nowadays the protection they offer to a typical computer is minimal; criminals concentrate on attacks that bypass firewalls. Therefore, your main recourse is to participate in the arms race, by applying to the software you're running all published security fixes. For most popular programs this is done automatically. Every so often the program contacts its vendor, and will inform you that a version that fixes some security problems is available for installation. What you need to do is to enable the automatic updates (you often get asked when you're installing a new program), and give an affirmative response when an update procedure asks you whether you want to proceed with an update.

13. Privacy

13.1 Get over it

There's an inevitable tension between privacy and convenience. For instance, if you receive personal email at work, your company can probably access its contents. You're thus giving up the privacy of your personal email for the convenience of reading it from your work account.

Over the last decade the scale has tipped toward convenience. Your personal data are probably already scattered among businesses and government departments all over the globe. This provides you more streamlined shopping experiences and less painful interactions with your government. Getting the jinn back into the bottle is impossible. Unless you choose to live like a hermit, relax, follow the measures I outline in the other sections, and enjoy the ride.

13.2 Think before you post

Perhaps you don't realize it, but the biggest threat to your privacy doesn't come from data you submit as part of a transaction to businesses and other organizations, but from data that you post for everyone to see in various blogs, forums, and social networking sites, such as Facebook, Twitter, LinkedIn, Google, and Flickr. A lot of this information is publicly visible, and can often even be located through a Google search. Employers, romantic encounters, friends, colleagues, relatives, even the parents of your children's' friends may run a search on your online activities to see if there are any skeletons in your closet. So, before posting a comment or a picture on a public forum, or joining a group or cause on a social networking site, think if you're comfortable sharing it with everybody on the planet, and if you'll still feel OK about it in five or twenty years (see also item 4.1).

13.3 Browse privately

We wouldn't want to share everything we do on the internet with our friends and family. You might be looking for marriage proposal ideas, shopping around for a surprise gift, looking up the symptoms of what could be an unwelcome disease, or tracing the career of your high-school love. Having these pages appear on your browser's history or auto-complete while you share your screen through a projector could be embarrassing or worse (see item 13.8).

Thankfully, modern web browsers have a private browsing mode (cynics call it porn mode), which lets you browse the web without leaving traces on your computer. The corresponding menu command for the various web browsers is *New incognito window* for Chrome, *Firefox – New Private Window, Tools – InPrivate Browsing* for Internet Explorer, and *Safari – Private Browsing*.

When you browse in private mode your browser will also provide considerable fewer personal details to the sites you visit. This can be useful when you want to see how a page, such as your profile or a web search, will appear to third parties. Needless to say, that once you log into a site while in private browsing mode, you're linking again your profile with your browsing trail.

13.4 Encrypt sensitive data

You may misplace a CD containing a backup of your files, you may forget a memory stick plugged on another PC, or your laptop may get stolen. In short, your files may turn out at the wrong, even criminal, hands. Make sure that the corresponding damage is minimal, by encrypting sensitive files. Such files could be the mails you exchange with your bank, your health records, the hot email exchanges with your lovers, your filings with the tax authorities, or even those family photographs you took at a nudist beach.

Keep in mind that the passwords you have for using your computer can't deter a moderately sophisticated criminal, because they're easily bypassed by starting up your computer with a special CD or memory stick. However, if you're using Windows and your files are located on a disk with a format called NTFS, you can encrypt complete folders by right-clicking on the folder name, and then selecting *Properties – Advanced – Encrypt contents to secure data.* If you follow this procedure, also choose a good password for logging into Windows (see item 12.6); if your password is easily guessable then your files are not really secure.

Another possibility is to use a program whose purpose is to encrypt data, such as the free program TrueCrypt (continued as TCnext).[1] An advantage of TrueCrypt is that it lets you keep bundles of encrypted files on external media, such as CDs and memory sticks. In both cases make sure you don't forget your password, otherwise the files will be as good as lost; there are no (known) backdoors that will allow you to recover your files.

13.5 Use strong encryption

Not all encryption schemes are created equal. Every so often a brilliant software vendor decides to encrypt data with the method that substitutes the letter K for A, L for B, M for C, and so on. Despite the venerable pedigree of this scheme (Julius Caesar protected military messages with it), you wouldn't want to encrypt your sensitive data with it, for any child can break it.

The encryption methods used in most office tools, such as WinZip (up to version 8), and Microsoft Word, Excel, and Access, are similarly insecure. If you doubt this, just type "excel password crack"

---

[1] https://truecrypt.ch/

on Google and marvel at the 1,490,000 search results. Therefore, if the secrecy of your data is important, avoid the toy encryption provided by these products. Instead, use the encryption method that your bank (hopefully) uses. It goes by the formidable name AES (Advanced Encryption Standard), and many software applications, such as TrueCrypt (see item 13.4) and 7-Zip,[2] use it to encrypt files. If you encrypt your data with such an application, and choose a good password (see item 12.6), and don't leave it lying around, you'll go a long way toward guarding your data's confidentiality.

13.6 Arrange for plausible deniability

The fact that only you know the password to some files you've encrypted doesn't mean they're entirely safe. In some jurisdictions you may be asked to reveal your password to investigative authorities or face charges. Worse, a criminal may force you to divulge your password at point blank, or a totalitarian regime may torture you in order to obtain it. If your life is so interesting that such circumstances can realistically arise, then you can give yourself some extra maneuvering room by setting up your data in a way that will keep your files secret, even if you reveal a password.

Specifically, programs, such as TrueCrypt (see item 13.4), allow you to put within the blank space allocated for your encrypted files, another set of files, encrypted with a second, different, password. Think of the setup as a safe box containing a secret compartment. Unless one knows this second password, it's impossible to tell that files are even located there; you can plausibly claim that you've not used that feature and that this is just blank space. (Hence the name "plausible deniability".) Take care however not to leave traces of these other files lying around, for instance on your word processor's list of recently opened files. In addition, when using this technique keep in mind that lying to a government agent regarding the existence of your hidden password can be a serious crime.

---

[2]http://www.7-zip.org

13.7 Don't encrypt more than you need

Encrypting your files, if you do it properly, is cumbersome. Not only do you need to carefully choose a strong encryption method and a good password, but you must also think about what happens to your files when you back them up and when you switch computers. More importantly, the more data you encrypt and protect the more chances there are that you'll be lax with the encryption and bring all of it to the open. For instance if you need to type a password to access each one of your files, it's more probable that at some occasion you'll mistype it in a place that will make it public. Then, all the files you've encrypted with that password will not be confidential any longer. Therefore, encrypt only what would really cause you problems if it fell into the wrong hands.

13.8 Consider your trails

The good thing about computers is that they can store everything we want. The bad thing about computers is that they will also store everything else. And by now you know that anything stored on a computer can get into the wrong hands. What can you do?

First, consider that there are two types of stored data. First, there are data stored on machines you don't control. The books you've bought on Amazon.com, the searches you've performed on Google, your friends listed on Facebook, the photographs you've uploaded on Flickr; the files you shared through Dropbox; the list goes on and on. There's not a lot you can do regarding such sites, other than to limit your online activities that can be traced to you (see item 4.1), and hope the sites you visit follow and enforce their privacy policies. Keep however in mind that if you've got trouble with the law, or you live under a regime that isn't known for its respect of human rights, then the range of your online activities that can be traced back to you increases considerably. For instance, even anonymous accesses to web sites can point to your person. In such cases, conduct your online activities at an internet cafe, without however using any sites or services that can be associated with you.

Then there are data stored on your computer. Your computer also keeps tabs on you. The details are difficult to clear and can be potentially embarrassing. For instance, you may have heard the story about the young lady who was surprised to find on her fiancé's web browser history a link to an online dating site. Once she opened the link, the browser helpfully filled in his alias and password. Armed with these details, she established her own identity on the online service, contacted him, and setup a date. I leave to your imagination the details of what transpired there.

For the casual examiner of your activities you might want to clear your web browsing history and the recently opened documents, both from the Windows *Start* or Mac Finder *Recent Items* menus and from all corresponding programs. The details vary according to the type and version of the operating system (Windows, Mac OS X, Linux) and application programs you use. However, you can easily find the specific sequences with a simple web search.

If you're really paranoid about the tracks you leave on your computer the easiest and most secure approach is to run your machine from one of those so-called Linux live CDs, such as the one for the Ubuntu Linux distribution.[3] These environments, in their default configuration, don't store anything on your hard disk. The moment you switch your computer off, everything goes away. This is rather inconvenient, so the dark secrets you're trying to protect should better be worth the trouble.

---

[3]https://help.ubuntu.com/community/LiveCD

13.9 Don't throw away your personal data

In 2007 Dr. Craig Valli from Australia's Edith Cowan University, and his colleagues bought used computer hard disks from various auctions, and examined the data they held. This was not the first time they were conducting such a study. Unsurprisingly, they found that a significant percentage of these disks contained sensitive personal and commercial data: bank account details, family photographs, strategic planning documents, confidential minutes, and letters to patients. Other data found was clearly embarrassing:

> "**Case29-AU** This was unformatted hard disk containing a 60GB NTFS partition from a religiously devout household due to the profile of web sites visited by various members of the family. There was no data of commercial nature found on the hard disk. However, it would appear that a young adult male in the house shaves their pubic regions and takes digital pictures of their erect penis for distribution via the Internet. This was substantiated by family photos found on the hard disk where the young adult male was featured clothed."

Some disks on Dr. Valli's sample came from organizations who should have known better: government departments, large corporations, banks, accounting firms, medical providers, and even the Information Systems School of an Australian University.

You can do better than that. Before you dispose a hard disk or a flash memory stick or card, run a full format on it (verify that the "quick format" option isn't checked). Even better, use a dedicated disk wiping program, such as *dban*[4] or *eraser.*[5] If the hard disk is faulty,

---

[4]http://dban.sourceforge.net/
[5]http://www.heidi.ie/eraser/

and you get along with tools, you can disassemble it, and (properly) dispose its various parts in different trash bins. And, never ever, post naked photographs of yourself on the internet, especially if you've got political ambitions.

14. Digital Preservation

14.1 Backup your data

In this true, 20-year old story, I've only changed the names of the individuals involved. Alice, working at a large service sector company, called their software vendor. "I'm afraid we just deleted the database of our clients," she said. "Please open our software's manual on page 156, and read it out," Bob, who was answering helpdesk calls on that day, told her. Alice read out the terse sentence printed out in bold in the middle of the otherwise empty page:

> **"Make regular backup copies of your data, or you'll be sorry."**

"Do you have a recent backup of your data?" asked Bob. "I'm afraid no," replied Alice. "Are you sorry?" asked Bob again. "Yes," replied Alice. "Works as documented!" snapped Bob.

It does not have to come to that. Nowadays corporate data are looked after a lot better than hapless Alice's database. However, as we increasingly conduct our personal affairs in a digital world, the data on our smartphones, home computers, tablets, and personal laptops becomes equally (if not more) valuable and worthy to protect. Backup copies of your data are a necessity, not a luxury.

Whole folders get accidentally erased, laptops get stolen, all hard disks eventually fail, home computers get smashed by earthquakes or drown in floods. The list of how the world (following Murphy's law) will conspire against you to deprive you of your data is endless. Creating a regular backup copy of your data is your only recourse against Murphy.

First, decide how much data you can afford to loose: a day's worth, a week's, or a month's? This will determine your backup schedule. Then, schedule the specific date and time you'll perform your backup. For instance, this can be the end of the day, each Friday, or the first Monday of the month. Mark this on your calendar or make it part of your routine (or schedule it to be performed automatically); don't rely on your conscience to remind it to you, because this doesn't work. To perform your backup, copy all your files to a storage medium separate from your computer. Data processing centers use tapes, but for personal use a USB memory stick or a recordable CD or DVD disk is often an adequate alternative.

On Windows computers you can find the backup functionality under *Start – Control Panel – System and Maintenance – Backup and Restore*. On a Mac the corresponding functionality is provided by clicking on the *Time Machine* icon of the menu bar.

14.2 Store backups off-site

Now that you've invested the effort to make regular backup copies, make sure that they don't go down with your ordinary data in the event of an accident. Keep them as far away from your equipment as possible; in the industry the term used is "off-site", and it sometimes means far enough to survive a nuclear blast. In your case, keeping your backups under another roof is probably enough; after a nuclear attack on your home town, accessing your PowerPoint presentations will be the least of your worries. Thus, a dedicated drawer or box at the home of your parents or children (depending on your age), your in-laws (if you get on reasonably well with them), or a close friend is an adequate option.

14.3 Keep multiple backup copies

To guard against data corruption that you recognize after some time, as well as accidents during backup and restore operations, you should keep multiple copies of your backups. Recordable disks are quite cheap, so it's not unreasonable to use a new disk for each backup. If your data are so voluminous or the backups so frequent that you find that this is an unreasonable burden on your pocket or the environment, you can use USB memory sticks, re-writable disks, or even portable hard disks, but with care. Have a pool of such storage media (say 5–10) and use them in rotation. Every so often, (say every month and at least each year) take a medium out of the pool, and store it permanently. In this way, if a file gets corrupted and you backup that version, you'll probably be able to go back to another backup in order to locate it in pristine form.

14.4 Backups are backups

There are many technology solutions to guard your data against accidents. Feel free to use them, but don't skimp on backups. For instance, you can keep a copy of your files in a separate folder, or another computer on your network, or use so-called RAID disks that will retain your data even if one of the disks breaks down. However, none of these solutions will help you if your building's equipment gets fried by lightning. Real backups are stored off-site (see item 14.2).

Colleagues (who should actually know better) often tell me that keeping a copy of their data on a single external hard disk or USB memory stick is a reasonable alternative. Again, this will not help you if you backup a corrupted version of your files, or if the external disk breaks down while you try to restore your data. Real backups include multiple redundant archived copies (see item 14.3).

14.5 Online backups are also backups

If you're comfortable with trusting your data to a third party and paying a monthly fee, then an online backup service may be the thing for you. Companies that offer this facility will copy your files to their storage banks through your broadband internet connection. You can then restore your files over the web. Some are also offering to send you back a CD with your data—a rather roundabout way to write a CD, if you ask me. To locate companies offering this service, search on the internet for "online backup".

14.6 Backup your smart devices

The smartphones and tablets we carry with us accumulate many critical data: contact details, appointments, notes, lists, photographs. The small size, mobility, and steep price of these devices makes them quite vulnerable to theft and messy accidents. (A Google search for "iphone water" returns 740 million results, including a hoax story where iPhone users were told that an Apple software update had made their device waterproof.) To avoid the nasty shock when you discover that you've lost all your contact data and the photos of your daughter's first steps, ensure that the data you store on your phone or tablet stays safe.

An online backup service (see item 14.5) can be the most convenient option for ensuring the availability of the data you store on your smartphone or tablet: simply enable the option to synchronize the data with your device's mother-ship, such as Google (for Android devices) or Apple (for an iPhone or an iPad). Alternatively, you must regularly synchronize your device's data to a regularly-backed up personal computer.

14.7 Keep your data together

You can only backup your data effectively if you keep it all in one place. If your data are scattered around your desk computer, your laptop, your old laptop, a couple of USB memory sticks (one of them hanging on your cat's neck), and some CDs, then chances are that some of them will inevitably go missing. Therefore, choose one computer as your primary data store, and remember to always copy there the definitive version of all your data. Then make sure that you religiously backup that computer.

To keep things simple, minimize the amount of data located on other computers or storage media, keeping them clean, and (mostly) empty. If you must work on diverse devices consider storing the associated data on an cloud storage provider, such as Google Drive or Dropbox (see item 6.17).

Furthermore, put all your data under one directory. Again, through this measure, if you backup that directory, you'll know that you haven't left anything out. This directory can be the one titled *My Documents* (under Windows) or *Documents* (on a Mac), which most well-behaved applications use by default for saving your files. Inevitably, a few more bits and pieces of your data will be on your desktop or saved with each application. However, all these elements (including your documents), live in a folder named *"Users/Your Name"*. If you back that directory up (or all of *Users* if many people use your computer), you'll be quite safe.

14.8 Test your backups

A company was diligently keeping backup copies of their test data, instead of their valuable actual production data. Another was repeatedly using a single floppy disk (remember those?) for storing a backup set that required seven disks. A third one was backing up the application program, instead of its data.

As with any task, there are many ways in which a backup may turn out a dud. You may be backing up the wrong files, or using buggy software, or a finicky storage medium. You'll rarely need to access a backup (I resort to mine about twice a year), but when you do, it's the worst time to find out that the data you really need aren't there. So, every so often, try to restore a file from your backup.

A good way to test your backups is to create a sacrificial file on your computer, back it up, delete it, try to restore it, and verify its contents. This procedure ensures that you won't loose valuable data, and you also won't think that you restored a file from backup when it was already on your disk.

14.9 Take care of those pictures

You or your parents have somewhere in the house photograph albums containing pictures of older generations. Some of those black and white photographs may well be a century old. Will your great grandchildren be able to see your digital photos?

I wouldn't bet on it. The folders of digital photographs you store on your computer are a lot more flimsy than those thick photo albums. Computers break down, files are misplaced, social networking sites go out of business (yes, it will happen), laptops get lost, and, let's face it, you're not taking backups as often as you should. Even if you decide to commit your photos to paper, note that your printer's inks will fade out in a few years.

What can you do? Store copies of your digital photos as plain files on CDs. Don't compress them into zip files, and don't change their format from their default JPEG type by importing them into an image editing program. You don't know if in 100 years there will be programs around to read those formats. Choose high-quality writable CD media. Label the CDs and hand them out liberally to your relatives.

14.10 Choose long-lasting file formats

The Danish cartoonist Storm P. famously quipped: "It is very difficult to make an accurate prediction, especially about the future." Nevertheless, if you look at how difficult it is nowadays to read file formats that were in the past as popular as Microsoft's Word documents are today, you'll realize that the long term availability of your data is a haphazard affair.

If NASA ended-up unable to read data recorded at the 1976 Viking mission to Mars, what are the long term preservation chances of your files?

Actually, not that bad. Because your work probably involves common platforms and software, you can easily improve the longevity of your data by following two simple rules.

Avoid niche or proprietary file formats

If only applications from a single vendor can read your data, then its survival depends on the vendor's continued existence and whims. For instance, newer versions of Microsoft's PowerPoint program can't read PowerPoint slides created with the first versions of PowerPoint. If you must use a proprietary file format, because it supports some features you need, then be sure to export important files into a standardized file format (see the following paragraph). When in ten years you can no longer use the proprietary format, you'll at least be able to access the most important parts of your data.

Choose standardized file formats

The internals of standardized file formats are openly documented, and therefore many applications can handle them. Consequently, there are more chances that one of those many applications will survive in the long term, or that an enterprising soul will create compatible software. Examples of standardized file formats (ignore those you don't recognize) are: JPEG, SVG, PNG, TIFF, and Postscript for graphics, plain text (TXT), HTML, DocBook, and (maybe) PDF for text, MP3 for music, and MPEG for movies.

14.11 Test your data when changing equipment

In the late 1980s I used a program called Framework II for word processing and spreadsheets. With horror, on one of my computer upgrades I discovered that Framework refused to run, terminating with an error. This would mean saying goodbye to the many files I wrote over a decade. Fortunately, I was able to write a small program to correct the fault. Over the last two years at least 314 other people faced the same problem and downloaded the correction program from my web page.

Every time you upgrade your computer (and thereby also probably the software you're running) your data are at risk. It's quite possible that your new configuration will not be compatible with your old files or programs. Some new programs may not be able to open your old files, other programs may not even run on your new setup. Worse, your new computer may not support the storage or backup media you used on the old one, for instance 5¼" or 3.5" floppy disks. Finally, during the transition you may have forgotten to transfer important data. Program settings, your email address book, and anything else that you don't see as a file may have decided to stay behind at the comfort of your old machine.

Therefore, while your (t)rusted old friend is still there, verify that you can still open and process key representative files. For instance, try to open a document, a presentation, a complex spreadsheet, your email folders, a couple of diagrams, and one of your retained backups. If you have problems, you may need to go back to the old machine and get missing files or programs. For files that you can't open, try opening them on the old computer and saving them in a more compatible format. The format of the applications you now use is obviously the best choice, but other formats, such as plain text for documents, comma-separated values (CSV) for data and spreadsheets, and PNG/JPEG for images can also help you keep some of your data.

To guard against problems that take time to manifest, keep your old computer accessible for a month or two, until you're sure that your new setup works correctly. However, avoid the temptation of working on it, because otherwise you'll loose track of the definitive location of your data.

14.12 Separate personal from work data

Don't mingle your personal data, such as photographs, bank statements, and email exchanges with friends, with work data. There are many reasons for this.

- When you switch jobs you want to maintain access to your personal files, but it may be difficult to take data from your work computer with you.
- You have fewer expectations related to the privacy of files you store on work computers. Your employer can examine them, and they can also be entangled in legal proceedings.
- Putting work-related files on an (often less secure) personal computer can be a violation of your organization's policies. Famously, former CIA director John Deutsch might have compromised sensitive defense programs by transferring their files to unsecured computers that were used to access his personal AOL email and more controversial sites.

At the very least, keep your personal files under a separate folder, so that it will be easy for you to split them from your work files when you need to. Ideally, use your own computer for your personal life.

14.13 Consider the data of your reports

The advice in this chapter also applies to your associates who report to you. As an effective manager chances are that you've delegated

the handing of many documents to coworkers. However, along with
the delegation of responsibilities you also have to ensure that the
corresponding documents will remain accessible if a colleague one
day suddenly leaves for a competitor, or if her laptop gets stolen.
Those documents stored on a shared, regularly backed-up directory
on a server are safe, those living on a personal workstation or laptop
are a ticking time bomb.

14.14 Consider the data of your family

You can't expect all your family members, such as older parents
and younger children, to be as diligent with their digital data as
you (hopefully) are. Remember when your parents handed you your
carefully-preserved first grade copy-books (probably, because they
needed the storage space in the attic)? It's now your turn to preserve
their digital data or that of your children. Either setup a backup
procedure for them, or ensure that their files are stored on your
regularly backed up computer.

15. Business Travel

15.1 Packing list

There are some people who carry with them everything they might conceivably need, just in case they need it, and those who prefer to travel light. There are advantages to both approaches; ultimately, I think the best approach is the one you feel most comfortable with. (Guessing what I carry when I travel is left as an exercise to the reader.) Here is an all-inclusive checklist to pick and choose from, as your personal style dictates. Some of the items plug into your laptop's USB ports; these are those nifty all-purpose rectangular sockets on your laptop's sides.

Power adaptor
> You can buy a second one for travelling, to avoid disrupting the cabling in your home and office.

Foreign socket adaptor
> Essential, if you're traveling to a country with different power sockets.

Power splitter
> Comes in handy when you want to share the single power socket at an airport gate.

Computer security cable
> This steel cable attaches with a lock to the so-called "Kensington Security Slot" of your laptop. A loop at the cable's other end allows you to secure it on a table or another large object. Although it will only stop an opportunistic thief, it gives you some peace of mind when you're in a busy place, such as a

hotel meeting room or a coffee shop. You can also use the cable to (sort of) secure your bag by threading it through the bag's handle.

Car power adaptor

This is heavy, bulky, and expensive. Given that you can easily drive your car to a place with a power socket, this item is most useful on camping trips or on a boat lacking mains power.

Second battery

Remember to charge it before you leave. However, for long term storage keep it about 40% charged to maximize its lifetime.

Mouse

A mouse designed for travelling is smaller and lighter than its desktop cousins.

Foldable keyboard

If you haven't seen this contraption, this is how it works. The keyboard is made from soft plastic so that you can roll it into a small cylinder and pack it in your bag.

USB memory stick

Even better carry two. An old inexpensive one that you can pass around without becoming upset if you loose it, and a high-capacity one you can use for backups and storing large files.

Empty CDs and DVDs

Can be handy when you want to distribute big files to colleagues, or if you want to perform regular backups.

USB adapter cable

You can get a cable with adapters that connect to all possible USB devices. Some cables roll neatly into a spring-loaded spool. Useful for connecting your smartphone, music player, or camera to your computer. Test that the adapters match all your devices; if not you'll need to carry their corresponding cables.

Headset

Use it to make Skype phone calls. You can find headsets with a single earpiece, which are a lot more compact than the twin-earpiece alternatives. Alternatively, test if you can use your cellphone's Bluetooth hands-free earpiece with your laptop.

Earphones

To listen to music, watch videos, or play games. Noise-cancelling ones are a nifty though pricey accessory for long flights.

USB phone charger

You can get a phone charger that plugs into you laptop's USB port. This saves you from having to carry a phone charger with you.

USB light

This plugs on a USB port and clips onto your screen, lighting your keyboard. It can allow you to work in a darkened airplane, or at night without disturbing your partner.

Backup of essential files

If some files are essential to the purpose of your travel carry a copy of those with you. Make sure that the files are in a format, such as PDF, you'll be able to use with a loaned computer at your destination.

Backup of files created while away

Before packing for the return trip make a backup of the files you created on your trip. These may be the photos you took during your vacation, or files of work you completed on a 11-hour plane trip. Why risk loosing them?

Entertainment material

> The weight of your laptop is considerable, and this doesn't even include all the paraphernalia discussed in this section. Make your laptop work harder during your trip by storing on its disk material that will make your travel a bit more enjoyable. This can include a movie you'd like to see, interesting articles worth reading, or music and audio books you'd enjoy listening to on the way or in your hotel room.

Laptop's warranty card

> If your laptop has a fast turn-around international warranty plan, carry the details with you.

Printed copy of essential notes

> Don't rely on your smartphone or laptop for details that are essential for your trip, such as the address and phone number of your hotel, or the details of your e-ticket.

Copy protection dongle

> If you're using software that requires a USB dongle to operate, take it with you.

USB hub

> A USB hub allows you to connect more USB devices to your laptop when its free ports run out. You'll probably need it if you pack and use everything in this list. You can get miniature travel hubs whose connecting cable folds in the hub minimizing their clutter.

Laptop

> Yes, I once left with its bag empty; I realized my mistake when I tried to do some work on the train to the airport.

15.2 Carry a USB stick on you

Douglas Adams, in his book *Life, the Universe, and Everything* famously had a suitcase misplaced at the Athens airport reappear some years later in a galaxy at the end of the universe. Your lost suitcase will probably be reunited with you through a less circuitous route, but nevertheless, it's worth playing safe and keeping your valuable data *on* you.

Before leaving for a trip, save your most valuable data, such as your presentation or the photos you took, on a USB memory stick and arrange to carry it on you. You can hang the USB stick by a lanyard around your neck, you can attach it to your keys, or you can slip it in your pocket. Just make sure that it's not located in the same bag as your laptop. Thus, if your laptop goes missing (lately, people carrying valuable personal data seem to have developed a habit misplacing theirs) you'll still have the data.

Yes, USB sticks on key holders and lanyards are slightly geeky, but when traveling we have to accept worse indignities. Finally, remember to remove the stick from your pocket, before putting your trousers into the washing machine. Some USB sticks have survived this ordeal, but don't bet that yours will too.

15.3 Backup before you travel

A colleague was leaving for a business trip, and didn't have time to backup his laptop at the office. So, he decided to take from his office the external hard disk he was using to store his backups, and perform the backups at home, before leaving. Unfortunately, (for in backup war stories, there's always an "unfortunately") his car was burglarized at a brief stop on the way home, and the thieves went away with his laptop and the (older) backups. Many years later, my colleague still remembers his misfortune, and still laments about the three months of work he lost.

Don't let this happen to you. Perform a full backup of the laptop you're taking with you two days before the trip. (Why two days? So that if something goes wrong with the backup procedure, you'll get another chance to repeat it.) During the trip backup the work you're doing on a USB memory stick, and keep the stick on you—separately from your laptop. This includes the digital photos you took. Two friends lost all their honeymoon photos when (unfortunately) they forgot their camera in a cab. Finally, immediately after the trip, perform again a full backup to secure the data you gathered during the trip.

15.4 Phone through Skype

Skype's ability to talk to other Skype users for free can be a major cost saver when you're traveling. However, many of your colleagues, friends, or relatives may not be available through Skype. For a modest cost Skype's paid service allows you to call any phone number around the world from your computer. With internet connectivity freely available in many places, Skype calls can be a bargain, especially compared to the exorbitant prices that hotels charge for phone calls and mobile phone operators charge for roaming. It can often even make sense to pay your hotel's (steep) internet access price, and then make all your calls through Skype.

15.5 Don't rely on network access

True, being able to access the internet on your travel can make your trip a lot easier, but don't rely on it. The hotel's internet service may be down, a connection at an airport lounge may act up, and your cell phone may refuse to roam. Therefore, ensure you've saved to your local disk everything you might need during your trip that's available online: maps, local information, sightseeing guides, contact details, business documents, etiquette cheat sheets, meeting schedules, and so on.

15.6 Arrange for network access before you leave

Often there's a dramatic cost difference between the price of network access you've arranged beforehand with your local telecom or internet service provider and that which you can purchase at your hotel or airport lounge. Before you leave, shop around.

15.7 Ask your hotel for a power brick

It's easy and also frustrating to forget or misplace (see item 16.4) your laptop's power supply or phone's charger when you're on a trip. Rest assured that you're not the first one to make this mistake. So walk down to your hotel's reception and ask politely if they have a replacement. It's quite likely that another customer may have forgotten a compatible power supply a few days (or months) before, which the reception might be happy to lend you.

16. Dealing with IT Equipment

16.1 Don't buy more than you need

Shelling out extra money for a top-of-the-line computer isn't as ludicrous as buying Brooklyn Bridge, but it comes close. Because the computing equipment is constantly evolving at a tremendous pace, the most expensive equipment is always targeted at the so-called early adopters—a polite term for people who can be easily separated from their money. The flip side of the coin is that you can buy equipment that is a year past its introduction date at a bargain price. So, avoid top-of-the-line equipment, unless you want to impress your children and their friends. (Let's face it: nowadays these are the only ones that your splashing on flashy equipment will impress).

In other types of equipment we often justify buying something more than we need, in order to cater for our future needs. In computing this argument doesn't hold water. First, unless you play graphics-intensive games, it's unlikely you can find today any computer that won't satisfy your computing needs for the next five years. In addition, by the time those unspecified additional needs actually materialize your computer will be obsolete. Therefore, buy exactly what you need today, and set aside the extra money for buying a more powerful machine when you actually need it. In computing, never buy today what you'll need tomorrow.

Finally, don't ever base your buying decisions on upgrade paths. Salespersons trying to sell you a specific model, because you can add an extra processor or more memory, are doing their job, but they are also being disingenuous. When you will actually need to upgrade their offering, those upgrade components will either not exist anymore, or will be pricier than a more powerful new computer.

16.2 Consider noise, space, and weight

Computer ads typically tout the stupendous speed and storage capacity of their offerings. However, unless you're running on your computer nuclear weapon simulations, 3D action games, protein folding experiments, or special effects for Hollywood movies, the power of any modern computer is more than adequate for your everyday needs. What's often not advertised is the computer's noise (from its various fans and disks), the space it takes, and (for a laptop) its weight. Yet with your computer being part of your everyday life these factors are important. A computer's noise can bring you headaches and hinder your concentration, while a heavy laptop can make your chiropractor your best friend. On the other hand, a small, sleek, and silent computer can adorn even your living room. Therefore, before buying a computer, ignore the gigabytes and gigahertz figures focusing on looks, noise, and weight.

16.3 Make your phone a Wi-Fi hotspot

Maslow's famous hierarchy of needs looks like a pyramid, starting with our basic physiological needs at the bottom (food, water, sleep), continuing with safety (of body, employment, family, health), and moving upward to levels describing our needs associated with love, esteem, and self-actualization. A witty hand has scribbled "WiFi" at the pyramid's foundation. The truth is not far away, because all the marvelous gadgets that have become an indispensable part of our lives tend to become shiny expensive bricks when they lack internet access. Having each laptop or tablet equipped for mobile data and paying a data plan for it can get expensive. Fortunately, there's often a better solution.

You can often turn your mobile phone with a data access plan into a personal Wi-Fi hotspot, so that your other devices can connect through it to the internet when you're on the road. You first need to turn on this functionality. On Android devices you do that by checking *Settings – More – Tethering and portable hotspot – Portable Wi-Fi hotspot*. Before you do that you need to give your hotspot a name so you'll recognize it (like "Jane hotspot") and a password so that others can't use it. These two settings are available under the *Portable Wi-Fi hotspot settings* option. On an iPhone the same functionality appears under *Settings - Cellular – Personal Hotspot*. Then, on the laptop or tablet that you want to connect to the internet, search for Wi-Fi networks, select the name of the Wi-Fi network you configured, and type in the password you gave. You should then be able to surf the web!

A few words of warning. The data you use through the hotspot counts toward your phone's data plan. Therefore, be careful on how you use it. Checking your email and your next flight should be fine, but it's probably not a good idea to watch videos, reorganize your email folders, or download huge files. The Wi-Fi hotspot feature consumes a lot of power, so it may be wise to plug your phone to a power source, and turn the feature off when you don't need it. Finally, note that some carriers disable this feature or require you to upgrade to a more expensive data plan in order to use it.

16.4 First unplug the mains plug

The second most frequently lost thing on Earth is a laptop's power supply. (The most frequent one is, of course, that other half of a socks' pair.) The story goes like this. When a meeting is over you're only too happy to be able to leave, or angry at what transpired there, or bored to death, or in a hurry to go home, or sleepless from the trip that brought you there. With your half-working mind you remove the cables dangling from your laptop, say goodbye to a colleague who is managing to leave before you, pack your laptop in your bag, and leave. When you unpack, you realize that your laptop's power brick is still in the meeting room's floor a few time zones away.

To avoid this unpleasantness and associated cost, make it a habit to always unplug the power supply's main cord before unplugging the power supply from your laptop. After unplugging the mains cord, pick up the power brick from the floor where you can forget it and place near your laptop, so that you can pack it immediately after unplugging the cord's other end. Each part of this little dance naturally leads to the next, so it's much less likely to forget a step.

16.5 Don't leave stuff around your laptop's keyboard

... because you'll probably smash its screen when you fold it in a hurry.

16.6 Desk phone on your right, coffee on your left

This prevents the handset's chord tripping the coffee mug, thereby treating your keyboard with your morning coffee.

16.7 Sleep, stand by, hibernate

By "hibernate" I don't mean that you should sleep over the whole winter like a bear, although in some areas this seems like a good idea. Most laptops, and increasingly also many desktop systems, offer you through the *Shut Down* command an option to *Hibernate* your system, instead of shutting it down. This preserves your desktop and all the applications in exactly the state you left them, by saving them to the hard disk. Also, the computer will start a lot faster when you turn it on.

There's also often a similar option called *Stand By* or *Sleep* that will resume the computer to the state you left it in seconds. This option, however, uses a bit of electrical power to keep the state of your applications, and can therefore either exhaust your laptop's batteries or loose your data if the mains power fails on a desktop system.

16.8 Don't rely on obsolete equipment

Riding on the fast-moving wave of computing technology is great, especially if you're a gadget fan. Every year you can buy cooler toys for less money. However, as with all waves, if you miss one, the next one may come and drown you.

In the case of computers this means that you don't want to get caught using obsolete equipment. If you're still using those 5¼" floppy disks, and your floppy disk drive breaks down, good luck to you. The only places you'll be able to find a replacement are flea markets and eBay, and you'll have to install it on your own. The same goes for many other devices, such as those that attach to your computer with special hardware (instead of a USB cable), or those that need their own software CD (the so-called "driver") to function. Chances are that if your computer breaks down and you upgrade it to newer software or hardware, you may be unable to use those devices.

Therefore, don't rely on anything that's more than four to five years old. Be thankful while it works, but be prepared to part from it without warning. And this means you should stop using those 5¼" floppies.

16.9 Use a second monitor

A second monitor on the desk isn't anymore a luxury reserved for traders and uber-geeks. You can probably easily afford it, and, if your work involves processing multiple documents at the same time, the investment will quickly pay itself through your increased productivity. For instance, if you work on a document, a spreadsheet, or a graphics design, you can also have the text with the relevant specifications or comments open on the second screen; no more tedious switching from one document to the other. Or you can reserve one screen for email and web browsing and the second one for document editing.

Before buying a second monitor ensure that your computer hardware supports it. You can plug-in the extra monitor into a so-called "multi-head" video card, into the external display port of your laptop, or into a second video card installed on your desktop computer.

16.10 Invest in a broadband connection

If you're still using a dialup connection to access the internet (3 million homes in the US at the end of 2012), put this book away, and purchase a so-called broadband connection. It will change the way you communicate and use the internet. The connection doesn't have to be fast, even the cheapest option will be ten times faster than your dialup access. The main advantage of the broadband connection is that it's always on. Therefore, Wikipedia, Google, Skype phone calls, your email (not to mention the various internet time wasters) are always one click away. No more idle minutes waiting for your modem to connect. When I got a broadband connection at home I found that it's more efficient for me to search for something online than to look it up in a book that's on the bookshelf across my desk. Quite a feat, if you ask me.

16.11 Wire your house

Although wireless networks are neat, they can't match the capacity, reliability, security, and performance of their wired cousins. Wired networks also simplify the extension of a wireless network's range with a so-called repeater. Therefore, when you renovate, rebuild, or build a house, arrange for network cables to go from a central location, such as a closet, the attic, or the basement, to each room of the house. Two such cables should go to every room and terminate to a special network socket. At the point where all cables end you will place what is called a switch and your broadband router. This arrangement allows all your household to share (or fight about) a broadband connection (see item 16.10), digitized photos, music, and films (see item 19.5), and a printer. This network also gives you flexibility to play or work in any room you like.

16.12 Reduce clutter through hubs

In computing terminology a hub is box that allows you to connect many cables together. By placing hubs in strategic locations (say under your desk or behind your printer) you can reduce the cable clutter that plagues most computer installations.

Say you want to connect to your laptop a printer, a keyboard, a wireless mouse, a scanner, your camera, a USB memory stick, a headset, and an external hard disk. You can plug all cables that can fit, spaghetti-style, to your laptop, and juggle with the rest, or you can use a couple of USB hubs. Place one hub under your desk, and connect to it the devices you need near you: keyboard, mouse, headset. Tuck away a second hub on your shelves where you have the rest of your equipment, and connect it to the first hub and to all the other devices. This neat setup allows you to connect all your stuff to your laptop with a single cable, and keeps your desk clean.

You can play a similar trick with network hubs and equipment, but if you have so many network devices in one place that they need a separate hub, you probably already know that it's needed.

16.13 Consider a printer's cost per page

Don't let a printer's rock-bottom price dazzle you into buying it. Low-end printers are sold following the so-called razor-and-blade business model, whereby the low cost of a razor (printer) is recovered from the high recurrent cost of the razor-blades (ink or toner cartridges). The price differences between printers and their ink cartridges have at times been so skewed that people where buying printers just to get hold of their ink cartridges. At some point manufacturers wizened up, and began selling their printers with half-empty "demonstration" cartridges.

Therefore, if you print more than a few dozen pages a month, base your decision on which printer to buy, not only on the printer's price, but also on the cost of its consumables over its lifetime.

16.14 Choose appropriate service and extended warranties

Although declining an extended warranty or service plan on your computer may sound like placing a bet that your equipment won't break, the truth is that you can cut corners in a rational way.

Here are some factors to help you decide. First, there are things that can easily break, and things that are a lot more resilient. Anything with moving parts (fans, hard disks, printers) and anything handled by children will eventually break, so a service plan for such a device makes more sense than one for, say, your broadband router, which is typically hidden away and solid like a brick. Laptops are also a good candidate for a warranty extension as they break down more often than their desktop brethren. This happens, because they suffer more abuse accompanying you on the road, and also because they're more flimsily built. Furthermore, the replacement parts for a laptop often come at an outrageously inflated price, because they are custom built for one vendor.

On the other hand, desktop systems are quite sturdy (until you pour your coffee into them), and any competent technician can easily fix them using standard off-the-shelf parts. Consequently, you can often save the money you'd pay for extending their warranty, and spend it if and when the need arises.

Finally, when planning ahead on what to cover, take into account who will pay for each option (repair versus service plan), and how difficult it will be to obtain authorization to pay for a repair if something that's not covered by a service plan breaks down. Sometimes you can allocate a warranty extension into a more convenient budget than that of an emergency repair. Also, in some organizations it's so difficult to pay for anything you've not budgeted ahead of time, that a service contract is the only way you can ensure that your equipment will not fall into disrepair.

16.15 Remove batteries after swimming

Powered electronics and water don't mix together. The electricity flowing through them causes nasty chemical reactions, which will corrode the delicate circuits beyond repair. Therefore, when you fall into a swimming pool with your tablet, pour coffee into your laptop, or drop your smartphone into a (hopefully freshly flushed) toilet, the best thing you can do is to immediately remove the device's battery. If the battery can't be removed, turn the device off, by holding down its power button.

Most electronic components come in sealed packages, and can therefore withstand an occasional accidental plunge, if unpowered. Remove as much water as you can by swiveling and rocking the device. Afterwards let it dry for several days in a warm (up to

60°C, 140°F) place. A hair-drier can also help, as long as you don't overheat the device. If the equipment is expensive or irreplaceable it's probably worth asking a qualified technician to disassemble it and properly dry its innards. Replace the batteries only after the device is completely dry. Putting anything electronic into a microwave oven is a really bad idea; such an action will literally fry it.

Finally, next time, before you visit the toilet remove your gadgets from you pockets.

17. System Administration

System administrators are the professionals in charge of feeding and caring the computers. They are responsible for setting them up, upgrading them, installing new software, fixing problems, and, of course, performing regular backups (see item 14.1). You shouldn't have been reading this chapter were it not for the fact that if you have your own computer, then you're probably its system administrator, unless you've found somebody to offload this task to (hi mom, hi dad, hi kids).

At work your IT equipment is (hopefully) managed by "real" system administrators. Remember to send them a thank-you card on the last Friday of July, the System Administrator Appreciation Day. If the organization you work for is too small to have a dedicated system administrator, then chances are you're also in charge of your work computer.

17.1 Log your changes

A diary detailing your interaction with your computer can save you many frustrating hours. This is not your childhood variety stuff.

> Dear Diary,
>
> Today I visited a very interesting web site...

Instead, in your diary simply write all the changes you make to your computer's setup: the installation of new programs and drivers, updates, option changes, and responses you provided to various tricky questions that invariably crop up during software installations. If you decide to keep the diary in electronic format, a simple document or spreadsheet located on your desktop will do just fine. (I keep mine as a simple text file, but a word-processing document also allows you to paste in it screen dumps of forms you filled-in—press *Alt-PrtSc* (*Ctrl-Shift-3* on a Mac) to copy an image of the window you're working on to the clipboard.) Remember to back up your diary together with the rest of your files.

This diary serves two purposes. First, by following it from the beginning, you can reliably recreate your working setup on a new computer. In addition, when a problem resurfaces (they invariably do) you can go back to your diary and see how you solved it the previous time.

17.2 Keep these installation disks

Over the lifetime of your computer many CDs will pass through your hands. The disks that came with your computer (or, if your manufacturer was too cheap to supply them, those you were prompted to create when you first turned it on), the disks that came with your printer, your scanner, your camera, your music player, your dog. They pile up. Keep them in one place, because if you ever need to setup your computer from scratch you'll need every one of them.

17.3 Upgrade before the EOL

Computer companies use the creepy term "end of life" (EOL) to refer to the time when they stop supporting a product. Reaching the EOL of a software program or hardware system can be bad news, if this is critical to your operation and difficult to replace. When, inevitably, a problem occurs you may have to find your way out on your own. For hardware using off-the-shelf components and open source software, you may be able to hire an expert to solve the problem for you. In all other cases you may end up having to solve a tricky problem under pressure. Therefore, it makes sense to upgrade or replace systems before these reach their announced EOL.

Of course, for systems that aren't critical and are also easy to replace (say a laptop used only to access the web) you can save money and effort by taking you chances, and riding those poor willing horses to death.

17.4 Save money and hassle with open source software

Open source software is distributed with a license that allows free redistribution and unrestricted use, as well as access to its internals (the so-called "source code") and the creation of derived works. Using open source software on your personal computer spares you the cost of commercial offerings; you may also want to install such software at work to avoid the paperwork and delay of the corresponding expense's approval. Furthermore, because any programmer can see and modify an open source software's code, such programs, in contrast to other freeware, won't push you obnoxious ads or sneakily pull your personal data. Well-known, mature open source software you might find useful includes the Libre Office[1] personal productivity suite, the Mozilla Firefox[2] web browser, the Mozilla Thunderbird[3] email application, the GIMP[4] image manipulation program, the Inkscape[5] graphics editor, the Audacity[6] software for sound recording and editing, and the FreeMind[7] mind-mapping software.

---

[1]http://www.libreoffice.org/
[2]http://www.mozilla.org/en-US/firefox/
[3]http://www.mozilla.org/en-GB/thunderbird/
[4]http://www.gimp.org/
[5]http://www.inkscape.org/
[6]http://audacity.sourceforge.net/
[7]http://freemind.sourceforge.net/

Another famous piece of open source software is the Linux operating system. In most cases your computer will have a pre-installed system (typically Microsoft Windows, Apple Mac OS X, or Google Android), and it would make little sense to replace it with Linux. However, if you want to breath life again into an old computer that's no longer supported by commercial operating systems, you might want to try installing the popular Linux-based Ubuntu[8] software distribution.

---

[8]http://www.ubuntu.com/

18. Ergonomics

18.1 Beware of laptops

A laptop is an ergonomics nightmare. Its worst aspect isn't the small size of its screen and keyboard, but the fact that the two are firmly joined together. Therefore, you can either place the keyboard at the height of your elbows and hurt your neck by bending it to look at the screen, or place the screen at the height of your eyes and wreck your wrists by having them flexed in order to reach the keyboard.

Furthermore, as Yefim Sheynkin and his colleagues at State University of New York at Stony Brook have demonstrated (don't ask), men using laptops on their laps elevate their scrotal temperature, which may negatively impact their fertility. Therefore, minimize the time you spend with your laptop in its bare state to the absolute minimum. In the places where you perform most of your work (say your office or home) arrange for a proper keyboard and mouse setup (see item 18.2).

18.2 Build a docking station

A docking station is an absurdly expensive kit that converts your laptop into a desktop computer, by adding to it extra ports and devices. Yet it's quite easy to build an affordable one on your own, and thereby make your laptop a lot more usable. First, buy a keyboard and a mouse, preferably with so-called USB connectors, so that you can plug them directly to your laptop. Place the keyboard and mouse at a height in which you can use them with your elbows at a right angle. Then, put the laptop on a stand (or a box, or a pile of books) so that the screen is at the level of your eyes.

To reduce the number of cables you have to plug and unplug every time you dock your laptop you can connect the keyboard, the mouse, and all your other devices, such your printer and broadband modem, to a USB hub (see item 16.12). Then, you'll only have to plug that into your laptop.

If you can spare the cash, also buy a larger screen and connect your laptop to it. If you plan this ahead, you can save some money (and your back), by buying a lighter laptop with a smaller screen—a screen you'll only use on the road. Finally, you can further reduce the weight you carry from your home to the office by purchasing an extra power supply unit, and keeping one at each place. Just remember to pack it with you, when you leave for a trip.

18.3 Remove your chair's handles

The handles of the chair you use in front of your computer are worse than useless. Unless they're adjustable, when you try to come near your keyboard, by bringing your chair under your desk or by sliding a keyboard tray toward the chair, the handles will invariably get in your way. They thus cause you to extend your elbows and prevent you from keeping them relaxed at a right angle. The solution is easy: remove the handles. I've done this in four offices I've occupied up to now, and I've enjoyed it every time. All you need is (typically) a hex key, and five minutes of your time.

18.4 Use keyboard shortcuts

A keyboard shortcut replaces cumbersome and time-consuming mouse operations. Why go through the menu sequence *Edit – Undo*, when you can simply press *Ctrl-Z* (*Cmd-Z* on a Mac)? When you use keyboard shortcuts there are fewer reasons to lift your hands from the keyboard to use the mouse, thus lessening the strain on your shoulders and wrists. For sure, memorizing the shortcuts is hard and somewhat geeky. Yet, the return on this investment materializes within days.

Most programs display the shortcut associated with a specific action, beside the command's menu name (for instance, *Edit – Paste: Ctrl-V*). For specific time-saving shortcuts see item 10.3, item 5.8, item 7.19, item 18.7, and item 18.8.

18.5 Create your own keyboard shortcuts

You can decrease typing and mouse dragging by creating keyboard shortcuts for operations that you perform often. This means that you can instantly perform the operation you want, simply by typing the key combination you assign to each task.

For instance, on Windows, right click on any item on your *Start* menu and follow the sequence *Properties – Shortcut – Shortcut key*. Type there an unused key combination, say, *Ctrl-Alt-U*. From then on, that combination will open the corresponding program or folder. If the item you want isn't on the *Start* menu, you can add it there, by dragging it to the menu using the right mouse key. When releasing the mouse button, select the option *Create Shortcuts Here*.

Other programs offer similar capabilities. On Microsoft Office you can assign a keyboard shortcut to any command through the sequence *Office Button – (Program) Options – Customize – Keyboard shortcuts*. You can even *record* a sequence of keystrokes and commands into what is called a *macro* (*Developer – Code – Record Macro*) and then assign a keyboard shortcut to it. Thus, if you're in the business of mass-producing mystery novels, you can save hundreds of keystrokes by recording a macro to write "It was a dark and stormy night", and associating it with a keyboard shortcut.

18.6 Keyboard smarts

Here are some shortcuts that are available under most systems, including Windows, Apple (if you press *Cmd* instead of *Ctrl*), Linux, and Android devices.

Shortcut	Function
Tab	Move to the next form field or window element
Shift-Tab	Move to the previous form field or window element
Enter	Confirm current operation (OK)
Esc	Cancel current operation (Cancel)
Ctrl-A	Select all
Ctrl-C	Copy
Ctrl-X	Cut
Ctrl-V	Paste
Ctrl-Z	Undo
Ctrl-Y	Redo
Ctrl-F	Open a Find window
Ctrl-B	Toggle bold on selected text
Ctrl-I	Toggle italic on selected text
Ctrl-N	Create new document in current application
Ctrl-O	Display the Open File dialog
Ctrl-P	Display the Print dialog
Ctrl-S	Save the current document
Ctrl-W	Close the current document
Ctrl-Home	Move to document's beginning
Ctrl-End	Move to document's end

You can also select text by holding down the shift key while moving (using for instance the arrow keys) to the end of the corresponding text. Furthermore, when you're in a selection list, such as a list of files, country names, or fonts, you can quickly move to a specific element by typing its initial characters. For instance, when a web form asks you to select the country where you live, you can quickly move from Afghanistan to USA by typing U. Scrolling down the list would be almost as painful as flying the distance.

18.7 Windows shortcuts

If you use Windows, there are additional shortcuts that can make your life easier. Here are the most nifty ones.

Shortcut	Function
Del	Delete selected text or item
Ctrl-Left arrow	Move to the previous word
Ctrl-Right arrow	Move to the next word
Ctrl-Backspace	Delete previous word
Ctrl-F4	Close the document you're editing
Ctrl-F6	Switch between open windows
F4	Open a selection list
Alt-F4	Close the application you're running
Alt-Tab	Switch between open windows
Windows-D	Minimize all open windows and show the desktop
Windows-E	Open a file explorer window
Windows-L	Lock your computer's desktop
PrtScr	Copy screen image to the clipboard
Alt-PrtScr	Copy the image of the current window to the clipboard

18.8 Mac shortcuts

Here are additional useful shortcuts if you use a Mac.

Shortcut	Function
Cmd-G	Find next occurrence of the selection
Cmd-H	Hide current application's windows
Cmd-M	Minimize active window to the Dock
Cmd-Q	Close the frontmost application
Cmd-Space	Show or hide the Spotlight search field
Cmd-Tab	Switch between open applications
Cmd-"	Switch between an application's windows
Alt-Left arrow	Move to the previous word
Alt-Right arrow	Move to the next word

Shortcut	Function
F11	Hide all open windows and show the desktop
F12	Show / hide Dashboard
Ctrl-F2	Move focus to the menu bar
Ctrl-F3	Move focus to the Dock
Ctrl-F4	Move focus to the active or next window
Ctrl-F5	Move focus to the toolbar
Ctrl-Shift-Cmd-3	Copy screen image the clipboard
Ctrl-Shift-Cmd-4	Copy a selection to the clipboard
Ctrl-Shift-Power	Lock your computer's screen

18.9 Tile your windows

Modern monitors allow you to view at least two documents at the same time. Yet your windows are often arranged in a way that forces you to continously switch between the one and the other. You can avoid this by arranging them side-by-side. If these windows are part of the same application you can do this through the application's *View – Window – Arrange All* command.

18.10 Phone, email, chat

Don't chat online when you can send an email, and don't send an email for what you can settle with a quick phone call. Your objective is to save keystrokes.

Online chatting is a real wrist killer, forcing you to a frenetic typing speed as you try to match up the pace of the spoken word. Nowadays it's cheap and easy to setup a voice conference, using your organization's PBX or Skype. Whenever somebody invites you to an online chat, politely suggest a phone call instead.

Email has some advantages over a phone call: it's less intrusive, it allows you to respond whenever you want, and keeps a written trail of the exchange. (The last one can also be a disadvantage; see item

6.8.) Nevertheless, an argument over email is less efficient over the corresponding voice conversation. Therefore, if *you* call the shots, consider using your prerogative to interrupt the other person's work and ask for instant attention, by lifting the headset each time you're after a quick answer.

18.11 Use a headset

Balancing a handset on your shoulder with you head to keep your fingers free to type, is an admirable acrobatic stunt and also a sure way to injure your neck's vertebrae. Buy a headset and use this when you're holding a phone conversation while using your computer. A headset also comes handy in those long self-contradicting hold sessions: "please hold the line, your call is important to us". The headset leaves your hands free to work while your call slowly advances the long queue until it's answered by the organization's single hapless operator.

19. Computers in our Life

19.1 Exercise

And by this I don't mean sword-fighting on your PC or game console; unfortunately, the impressive feats you achieve there aren't reflected on your body. If you're reading this book, you probably spend too much time in front of a computer screen. Which means that the only muscles you exercise are those of your fingers. It's also likely that you stress other parts of your body, such as your back, your elbows, and your neck. Additional exercise will help you counterbalance your sedate workday and its associated stresses; stronger muscles will tolerate better the daily punishments your inflict on them in your office. Keep in mind that, like water, food, and sleep, exercise is not optional. It just takes longer for your body to start complaining. So, just as you make time to sleep every day, you must schedule non-negotiable time to exercise at least three times a week. Your body, and those who love you, will thank you for that.

19.2 Contribute to online communities

The internet has democratized the production of content. You can feel the joy of contributing to a common effort by actively engaging yourself in online communities. Here are some ideas.

- Correct typos or improve the wording in wiki articles, such as Wikipedia's or those in more specialized wikis
- Answer some newbie questions in an online forum you frequent

- Contribute a thoughtful comment to a blog entry
- Write an article in a blog or a wiki in area that interests you
- Participate in, or start a new Facebook group or cause
- Create your own blog

19.3 Avoid addictive endeavors

Many computer and internet–related activities offer us immediate gratification for our efforts. You type for an hour and you get a polished report; you post an interesting blog entry, and minutes later comments from around the world are piling in; you can become a published encyclopedian the day you first type wikipedia.org; you fool around with your joystick and you win a Formula-1 race.

This easily explains why these (and, unfortunately, too many other) activities can become addictive. So, keep a watch on yourself guarding against computer-related addictive behavior. No matter if this is spending hours looking at the photos of the friends of your friends on Facebook, or performing (doubtlessly educating) internet research on underwear models, when you sense that an activity is interfering with your work or real-world social life, stop it.

19.4 Rip your CDs

It's easy to convert the contents of a CD into a so-called MP3 compressed audio file that you can listen through your computer, smartphone, tablet, or portable music player. This procedure goes by the charming name of ripping. A program, such as CDex,[1] allows you to put an audio CD into your computer's CD drive and convert all its tracks into MP3 audio files. If you convert all your CDs into MP3 files, you can then store the files in one place (see item 19.5), and play them on your stereo through your computer (if this

---

[1]http://cdexos.sourceforge.net/

matches your living room's setup), or using a device called a *digital audio streamer.*

Through this process you protect the content of your CDs; some CDs turn brown with time and become unplayable. Young children are also notorious wreckers of irreplaceable CDs. You can also save space, because many shelves or drawers of CDs can fit into a single hard disk. Once you have ripped your CD collection you can move the CDs to a high inaccessible shelf, or hide them in your basement.

19.5 Centralize your media content

It makes sense to keep your digital photographs, music files, and movies under one roof. A dedicated computer ("server" in the industry parlance) to which all other computers tables and phones in your household can connect, allows you to share this content in the way a family shares its books, records, and magazines. For this purpose you can use an old computer (with a new large hard disk), or you can buy what is called a "network disk drive".

19.6 Digitize your kids' art

"Space: the final frontier" describes more than the world of Star Trek. It also describes our overflowing shelves, cupboards, and attics. Often, a considerable part of this space is often taken by our children's masterpieces — drawings, essays, exercise books — which their kindergartens and schools helpfully return to us by the truckload. Keeping all that stuff is untenable, throwing it away seems a shame, and giving it to charity simply doesn't work.

Here's a solution. Take a picture of that wonderful drawing or eye-watering essay, and save it on your hard drive. If you've read this book's chapter on digital preservation, and, more importantly, follow what it recommends, chances are that your young Einstein's

drawings and your budding Picasso's physics workbook will be
with you and your children for decades.

Epilogue

The famous science fiction writer Arthur C. Clarke wrote in his book *Profiles of the Future*:

> "Any sufficiently advanced technology is indistinguishable from magic."

This became known as his third law, and, inevitably, it gave rise to Gehm's Corollary:

> "Any technology distinguishable from magic is insufficiently advanced."

Having read the previous chapters, I'm sure you know where I'm getting at. Today's information technology is insufficiently advanced. Every annoyance, difficulty, bug, and stern warning you encounter is a sign of the technology's immaturity. The spam you receive, the need to backup your data, the tricks for searching documents and the web, the advice for organizing your files, your concerns for your privacy and security in the online world, the cables sprawling around your computer, the ergonomic problems you face in your interactions, and this whole book are all signs of deeper problems.

We still have a long way to go. However, until we get there, come to terms with the fact that computers are a very powerful yet insufficiently advanced technology. Use it to increase your productivity, hone your skills to make it work for you rather than against you, but don't blame yourself for its imperfections. This is an exciting journey; enjoy it!

Acknowledgements

- Cover design by Irini Karydaki
- Cover photo credit: My Rig[2] by Henry Hagnäs.
- Yiorgos Adamopoulos proposed item 12.4 and item 16.6, and also spotted numerous typos.
- Nikolas Koskoros and Vagelis Tripolitakis sent valuable fixes.
- Florents Tselai proposed item 2.14.

---

[2]http://www.flickr.com/photos/hagge/4573332241/in/photostream/

www.ingramcontent.com/pod-product-compliance
Lightning Source LLC
Chambersburg PA
CBHW071159050326
40689CB00011B/2178